"Losses by death are the most traumatic processes in our lives—but they can also be occasions of growth. I think that Sandi Caplan's and Gord Lang's protocol will be most effective in helping hurting persons grow through their losses. They used their extensive experience in facilitating grief groups to design a program which is second to none."

> —*J. W. Morgan*, Ph.D., King's College Centre for Education About Death and Bereavement

"Grief's Courageous Journey is a wonderful guide to healthy grieving!"

> —*Father Jack McGinnis*, Chaplain, The Meadows Treatment Center, Wickenburg, Arizona

"This workbook provides a compassionate guide, a suggested structure to help one through the disorienting maze of feelings engendered by loss. It reflects quite clearly the gentle yet strong support the authors give to those for whom they have been counselors."

> —*Beryl A. Chernick*, M.D., Ph.D., and *Avinoam B. Chernick*, M.D., F.R.C.S.C., authors of *In Touch*

"I would like to endorse, strongly, this publication as an extremely valuable guide to anyone going through the loss of a loved one."

> —*L. L. de Veber*, M.D., F.R.C.P.C., Director, Pediatric Hematology / Oncology; Professor of Pediatrics, University of Western Ontario

"Our volunteer facilitators of grief support groups depend on this valuable book and the model it provides."

> —*Cathy Walsh*, Executive Director, Bereaved Families of Ontario, London Chapter

"Grief's Courageous Journey has enhanced personal understanding of loss and the potential for healing. I can attest to this as one of the most personally insightful involvements in my teaching career."

> —*Peter Valiquet*, Coordinator of Family Life and Health Education, Catholic Schools of London / Middlesex, Ontario

Grief's Courageous Journey

A
WORKBOOK

SANDI CAPLAN & GORDON LANG

NEW HARBINGER PUBLICATIONS, INC.

Publisher's Note

This publication is designed to provide accurate and authoritative information in regard to the subject matter covered. It is sold with the understanding that the publisher is not engaged in rendering psychological, financial, legal, or other professional services. If expert assistance or counseling is needed, the services of a competent professional should be sought.

Copyright © 1995 New Harbinger Publications, Inc.
5674 Shattuck Avenue
Oakland, CA 94609

Cover art by Roman Tybinko, oil on canvas, 1985.
Cover design by SHELBY DESIGNS & ILLUSTRATES.
Text design by Tracy Marie Powell.

Distributed in the U.S.A. by Publishers Group West; in Canada by Raincoast Books; in Great Britain by Airlift Book Company, Ltd.; in South Africa by Real Books, Ltd.; in Australia by Boobook; and in New Zealand by Tandem Press.

ISBN 1-57224-018-0 hardcover
ISBN 1-57224-017-2 paperback

Originally published as *Grief: The Courageous Journey* by Cor Age Books, London, Ontario, Canada.

99 98

10   9   8   7   6   5

Contents

Preface

As colleagues in the Pastoral Care Department of St. Joseph's Health Centre, London, Canada, we had the opportunity to work with many people facing death and crisis in their lives. Being with them throughout part of their courageous grieving-healing journey, we came to appreciate the value of grief as a unique, personal response to a significant loss, whether it was loss of health, death of a loved one, or any of the important losses we face throughout our lives. We found a simple, down-to-earth way to help people effectively grow through their losses, and thus *Grief: The Courageous Journey* is a dream realized.

In 1989 we established Pathways to offer a variety of programs and resources designed to guide bereaved people through the process of mourning towards greater self-knowledge, strength, and ultimately a sense of renewal. The foundation of our approach to grief work is based on the belief that grief is neither an illness nor a pathological condition, but rather a highly personal and normal response to life-changing events, a natural process that can lead to healing and personal growth. The transition through this difficult time is the courageous journey. We firmly believe, however, that unacknowledged losses or unexpressed grief can continue to cause pain and contribute significantly to ill health, unease, and loss of purpose and meaning.

There are several components that we have found to be very important, if not essential, to the grieving-healing process. Principal among these are the needs to recognize the importance of our loss and to "tell the story"; that is, we need to review in detail in a completely safe and nonjudgemental context the whole relationship with the person who has died, and to express freely all the feelings to which the process gives rise. We also believe that it is important to have some knowledge of the grief process and grief work and an awareness that this process can take a long time and is unique to each individual.

Our workbook continues to be a safe place for many bereaved people to tell their stories and express their feelings. The workbook and the facilitator's guide are also used extensively as a framework for counselors, clinicians, social workers, teachers, clergy, palliative care and hospice volunteers, and other supporting people, individually or in groups, who are journeying through the grief process.

We hope that this book will help you on your courageous journey.

Acknowledgments

We gratefully acknowledge Barbara Novak for her encouragement, skills, insights, and sensitivity as our editor, and the hosts of other people who have encouraged our work and the publication of this book.

Sandi Caplan

In 1947, when I was two years old, my father, Nat Gurarie, died. I knew him as a loving, kind, and special person only through my memories and stories of family and friends, and especially through my mother, who had lost her best friend. In spite of the tragedy in her own life, my mother's strength and ability to overcome adversity helped her to create a normal, secure, and happy life for both of us. In 1949, she married again, and my sister Barb, to this day my best friend, was born.

It wasn't until the loss of my adoptive father, Harry Novak, that I understood that I was still grieving for the father I had lost as a young child, and that the feelings and fears of grief that I was too young to recognize and express at the time had been buried deep inside. Finally, 35 year later, I began my grief work.

Through my own experience and the experiences of many people who have allowed me to share their stories, I have learned that losses need to be grieved and that it's never too late to begin the grieving process. I have learned, too, that healing has been possible only with the help of the people in my life who have loved and supported me through the difficult times and who taught the two-year-old child I was the happy side of life. I dedicate this book to you.

I am particularly indebted to the following people who shaped my life and deeply influenced my work:

- The Levine family and all the friends who, so many years ago, provided hugs and laps for a confused little girl and encouraged me to laugh and play in the midst of pain and loss

- My mother, Sylvia Novak, who has taught me always to see life as a gift, and who continues to delight in living life to the fullest every day and despite all the difficult times she has faced in her life

- The many patients, clients, and friends who found in me "a safe place" to share their stories, thoughts, and feelings

- Friends and colleagues in the Pastoral Care Department of St. Joseph's Health Centre in London, Ontario, who taught me about spiritual journeys and the many roads to one's own truth, and in particular, Judith Soulliere, who recognized the quality of the program and had the foresight to have it documented

- My sister, Barbara Novak, whose enthusiastic support, advice, and insights have deeply influenced my life

- My partner, co-author, wise teacher, and gentle friend, Gordon Lang, who taught me about grieving and healing and whose capacity for warmth, love, and compassion created a safe place for me and the hundreds of others whose lives he has touched

- Adam and Mitch, my children, for their sensitivity and understanding well beyond their years, for the fun we've had, and for all that they have taught me

- And finally, Paul, my husband, who has provided a constant source of love and encouragement

Gordon Lang

On May 8th, 1995, I celebrated 65 years of living on planet Earth. They have been good years, although not without pain and tragedy. As I grow older I realize how little time we have together. Life is precious. Over the past 15 years I have been privileged to work with bereaved people of all kinds. They are beautiful people. They have been my teachers. I thank them all from the bottom of my heart. We are all students and teachers for each other.

When I was almost 50 years old and in the middle of a major mid-life vocational change, my father, and mother, and two younger brothers died, and two male cousins committed suicide. I thought I was going crazy. I had been a professional all my working life, but I knew nothing about grief. And no one seemed able to help me understand what was happening to me. I found my answers from widows and widowers in a "Good Grief" group. There I began my grief work, and it continues today. We never completely finish the business of grieving our life losses. The deepest life loss, in my opinion, is the loss of our true selves, the child within.

I have always wanted to provide a simple, down-to-earth, effective way for people mourning the death of a loved one. *Grief's Courageous Journey: A Workbook* is a dream realized. It comes out of raw experience with bereaved people, often in small grief support groups. I want to thank my partner, Sandi Caplan, for her determination, encouragement, and contribution. Without her, this book would have never been published.

In gratitude:

- To my wife, Joan, for her never-ending love, support, and encouragement

- To my family, Steiv, Diane, and Chris, for being there

- To my granddaughter and mentor, Charmaine Noel, for the wisdom of a child

- To my family of origin (the Lang-Hummel connection) for launching me into life

- To Cathy Walsh and Bereaved Families of Ontario (London Chapter) for educating me to the ups and downs of the grieving-healing process

- To doctors of the soul and body, Barrie de Veber, Graham Chance, Elizabeth Kubler-Ross, and Jack Morgan

- To the Irish Creation spirituality group, Matthew Fox, Fr. Paddy Green, and M. C. Richards, for stirring my creative juices

- To Twelve-Step folks, especially Adult Children of Addiction, for nudging me out of denial

- To a variety of men's groups for nurturing men's stuff within me

- To my psychodrama mentors, Rosita and Mary, for making me conscious of my unconscious control drama

- To the Resurrection Community who for thirty years walked with me in my early spiritual growth

- To Fr. Jack McGinnis, retreat leader, who inspired my own inner-child journey

- To all those who participate in psychodrama, retreats, and workshops with me (and Joan) for allowing us to witness how goodness grows in and through the courageous revelation of our deeply wounded inner spaces

Introduction

When someone close dies, it is normal to feel devastated—physically, emotionally, spiritually. It hurts to know that we will never again feel their closeness, be able to hug them, talk with them, cry with them. All our hopes and dreams seem to come to a crashing end. There are at least five components that we have found to be very important, if not essential, to the grieving-healing process. They are:

1. Recognizing the importance of our loss
2. Telling the story of our relationship with the lost loved one
3. Expressing our feelings
4. Finding a safe place to tell our story and express our feelings
5. Having some knowledge of the grief process and grief work

Finding a safe place

We cannot begin to understand what this means all at once. We are too confused and disoriented. There are too many feelings to deal with—shock, disbelief, anger, guilt, sadness, tears, depression, loneliness, powerlessness, fear, panic. . . . We can deal with only so much reality at a time. We need some protection, a safe place.

Perhaps you feel frozen, numb. Not until you feel the anguish and pain of your loss will the numbness give way to feelings. This is the grieving-healing process.

Grief work is exhausting, emotional work. Torrents of feelings can wash over you. Feelings of loneliness, loss of identity, loss of self-esteem; anger at yourself, others, the one who has died, God; fear of the future, fear of being unable to cope, fear for your own sanity—all these feelings can be overwhelming. They come in waves that knock you down over and over again.

It is important to deal with your own feelings at your own pace, slowly and gently, in your own time. Slowly you can come to realize that although a physical separation has occurred, a strong connection remains. You can come to "affirm a bond of love with your loved one that death cannot destroy."

Although you will miss your loved one for the rest of your life, you can learn to face your feelings and deal with them in a constructive way.

It is important to find a safe place to go over in detail the whole story of your relationship with the one who has died. *This workbook can be your safe place.* It will provide you with the opportunity to review, reflect, and remember all aspects of your relationship with your loved one, step by step, according to your own time frame. Be gentle with yourself.

Using this workbook

We suggest that within the first year of your bereavement you take six to ten weeks or longer to work through some of the feelings around your life loss. Note that this is only a beginning. Grief and healing are parts of a long process—not days, weeks, or months, but years.

You need to know there will be "trigger" events throughout the rest of your life. For example, you might see someone on TV who looks like the deceased; you might go to a wedding or graduation and break down; Christmas, Father's Day, Mother's Day, and anniversaries all can be difficult for a long, long time.

Healing is a life-long process towards human wholeness. All of us have hurts to be healed, life losses that may remain unrecognized until one significant loss drops us into a pit where we realize that we must deal with our grief. It is better to begin to deal with our grief feelings sooner rather than later—ideally within a month or two after the loss occurs.

We suggest that you purchase a notebook for additional pages for the workbook exercises and for use as a journal.

Journal writing

A journal is a safe space where you are free to express your deepest thoughts and feelings. It is accessible and private. No one else will read it unless you want them to. You can't hurt anyone's feelings and won't have to defend anything you write. Although you may feel blocked at times, you can come to trust yourself. The censor and inner critic will disappear in time.

A journal is a place to record your exercises, special memories, reflections, insights, and inspirational messages that come to you as you do your grief work. If you have never kept a journal, we suggest you try it. And remember, you share only what you want. It is for you.

Don't try to do your grief work alone. Choose a workbook partner, a trusted friend, a counselor, or a therapist who will listen to you as you recount all aspects of your relationship with the person who has died. Even better would be to find a small grief support group of similarly bereaved people with a skilled facilitator, perhaps through a church or community agency. Grief is confusing. It is easy to become disoriented. Other bereaved people can provide a point of reference. It is reassuring to know that others are going through the same feelings and behaviors that we are, that although we may be in grief, we are not "crazy."

Shared joy is double joy;
Shared sorrow is half-sorrow.

—Swedish Proverb

Part I

Understanding Grief

Grieving for Our Losses

Life losses

Any loss that causes a significant change to our lives is a life loss. Death is the most obvious life loss, whether it be death of parents, grandparents, children, relatives, friends, neighbors, or colleagues.

But other losses can be wrenching enough to cause the pain of grief. These life losses might include the loss of a relationship, job, pet, home, family farm or business, mobility, health, or memory.

And of no less significance, though perhaps less tangible, is the loss of some aspects of our belief system, such as loss of innocence, trust, respect, dignity, hopes, dreams, faith, or religion. These, too, are life losses.

Unresolved losses continue to cause pain

A recent loss may trigger feelings connected with past life losses. We may have said, "I'll deal with that some day." Now may be the "some day" when you are dealing with more than one loss.

> *When a person is born, we*
> *celebrate; when they marry we*
> *jubilate; but when they die we act*
> *as if nothing has happened.*
>
> —Margaret Mead

Your life losses

Make a list of all the significant losses you have experienced in your life. Note, as closely as you can, the year in which each occurred. In your journal, draw a line and mark it off at five-year intervals. Now chart your losses chronologically along the line. There are many ways to chart or draw your lifetime experience with loss so that you will be able to see it over your whole lifetime. Be creative and feel free to choose a way that works best for you. Your chart might look something like like this:

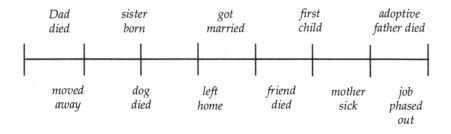

When you are finished, look for patterns on your chart. What is the first loss you remember? Notice if there are any periods when more than one loss occurred about the same time or were grouped in the same segment? You also might like to add any major decisions or changes in your life at the time of, or as a result of, a particular loss.

This is an opportunity to understand your history of losses and how they might be affecting your reaction to the loss you are experiencing now. However, doing this exercise can be an emotional experience. Circle on your chart the losses that caused you pain as you recalled them. They may be recent losses or unresolved losses from many years before that are continuing to cause pain. Be aware of what emotions are being aroused. When you are ready, use the space below to write some words to describe these feelings.

_____

_____

_____

_____

_____

_____

_____

_____

_____

_____

_____

_____

_____

_____

_____

_____

_____

_____

_____

If you working with a counselor or friend, share your chart with them and tell them about these significant times in your life.

What could you do to take care of yourself right now?

Grief

Grief is a highly personal response to life losses. Every relationship we have with a person is unique, irreplaceable, and unrepeatable. Since our relationships are unique, our grief is unique, too.

A husband and wife will each grieve differently when a child dies. Each member of a family will mourn the death of a parent differently.

There are no road maps, no blueprints for grief. After his wife died, C.S. Lewis, in *A Grief Observed*, set out to devise such a road map. He gave up the attempt.

It is always a mistake to judge how another person is expressing grief.

"He doesn't show enough emotion."

"She is just overreacting, crying all the time."

"He just carries on as if nothing has happened."

Instead of judging, we must be very patient and accept the uniqueness of every individual's grief process, including our own.

Your grief

This exercise is designed to help you become aware of your unique reaction to your loss and the reactions of others in your family as they deal with their own grief.

Some of the feelings often associated with grief are: powerlessness, fear, anger, and guilt. Other reactions are shock, disbelief, numbness, sadness, tearfulness, depression, sorrow, loneliness, isolation, panic, anxiety, frustration, and sleeplessness. These words may help you identify your feelings and reactions, or you may come up with different words entirely.

You might try writing with your nondominant hand. This is a way to "hear" your true feelings and let go of the need to "do this perfectly."

Find a comfortable position, sitting or lying down. Take a few deep breaths, as you clear your mind and focus your thoughts. You might want to close your eyes. As you review some of the losses in your life, begin to focus on one that was particularly significant, perhaps one that continues to arouse feelings. Take a few moments to think about this significant loss.

When you are ready, use the space below to write some words that describe how you have responded to loss emotionally.

_____

_____

_____

_____

_____

_____

_____

_____

_____

Describe how you have been acting/reacting since the time of your most recent loss (for example, crying, getting angry, withdrawing, and so on).

_____

_____

_____

_____

_____

_____

_____

_____

_____

_____

Now think about your family (spouse, children, close relatives) and describe how they acted or reacted to the loss.

_____

_____

_____

_____

_____

_____

_____

_____

_____

Each person in the family had a different relationship with the person who died, and therefore each person's grief response will be different. Describe any difficulties you and your family experienced as a result of your different reactions to your loss.

_____

_____

_____

_____

_____

_____

_____

_____

_____

_____

Picturing grief

Some people find it helpful to create an image of how they are feeling. Here are some examples that might help you create a picture of your grief.

Grief is like a jigsaw puzzle. Sometimes we feel like we have it all together. Then an accident happens. Our life falls apart. We try to put the pieces back together, but they don't fit any more. Our values, priorities, and outlook all have changed radically. We feel overwhelmed. We don't know where to begin.

Grief is like a broken heart. Who can mend it?

Grief is like a wound. Grief is a cut, a slash on our body. At first there is no feeling. We are numb. Then gradually we begin to hurt, to feel the pain. We have to tend the wound carefully to avoid infection. Proper rest and attention and time all help the healing process. Healing is a slow process. There will always be a scar. The scars of grief should be worn proudly because they are signs of how much we have loved.

Grief is like waves pounding on the seashore. At first the waves come in piled one upon the other, tumbling in confusion. Gradually they slow down. At first grief seems to knock us down every minute. Gradually there's more time between waves. We still get knocked down from time to time. Sometimes we can see the wave coming (such as at Christmas, a birthday, or a particular season of the year), and we can brace ourselves for it. Often the anticipation is worse than the reality of the actual wave.

Grief is like a maze. There are so many blind alleys. Where is the right passageway? Who is there to guide us, to give us safe conduct through this maze of feelings and emotions? How can we find our way through? It feels so confusing. We feel lost and alone.

Grief is like a stream. As we cross to the other side we go from stepping stone to stepping stone, often afraid we will fall and get carried away in the turbulence of the rapids.

Picturing your grief

To prepare for this exercise, find a quiet place and comfortable position. If you find it difficult to concentrate, try spending some time with your eyes closed, with or without music, and breathe slowly and deeply, focusing your thoughts on your breath. Let your mind empty of thoughts.

What image comes to you when you think of your loss? Use the space below (or your journal) to draw your image. Feel free to use words, pictures, lines, colored pencils, or markers to draw what your grief looks like to you.

Can you put words to the image you drew? If you need help finding the words, choose those that feel right for you from the list below and then add your own words in the space provided on the next page. You may want to refer to this list several times as you work through the exercises in the workbook.

AFRAID	ANGRY	HURT	POWERLESS
fearful	*resentful*	*injured*	*helpless*
frightened	*irritated*	*offended*	*numb*
timid	*enraged*	*distressed*	*in shock*
shaky	*annoyed*	*in pain*	*disbelief*
restless	*enflamed*	*suffering*	*lethargic*
doubtful	*provoked*	*afflicted*	*guilty*
awed	*incensed*	*worried*	*regretful*
dismayed	*infuriated*	*aching*	*shamed*
threatened	*offended*	*crushed*	*frustrated*
cowardly	*worked up*	*victimized*	*sad*
appalled	*cross*	*heartbroken*	*depressed*
quaking	*sulky*	*hapless*	*tearful*
menaced	*bitter*	*in despair*	*sorrowful*
in a panic	*boiling*	*agonized*	*isolated*
lonely	*fuming*	*tortured*	*sleepless*
isolated	*in a stew*	*piteous*	*exhausted*
not belonging	*wrathful*	*woeful*	*longing*
	indignant	*rueful*	*a failure*
		mournful	*emptiness*
		sad	
		pathetic	
		tragic	
		vulnerable	

Describe what your grief feels like to you.

_____

_____

_____

_____

_____

_____

_____

_____

_____

_____

_____

_____

_____

_____

_____

_____

_____

_____

_____

_____

_____

_____

_____

Grief is . . . is not

Grief is not an illness. It is not a sign of weakness, or a problem to be solved, even though it might feel like one and other people may treat you as though you are "sick" or have a problem.

Grief is not like a broken bone or a cold or an allergy. There is no "quick fix," no "easy cure" for grief. Nor are alcohol, drugs, food, sex, or work helpful when used as solutions to replace, deny, or avoid the pain of grief work.

Grief is a transition. It's a long, slow, time-consuming, painful, healing process, a journey towards human wholeness. This workbook is designed to guide you on your journey towards healing.

How long does grief last? People often think grief lasts for a few days or weeks. The intensity of feelings changes, but grief lasts more than months or even years.

The first year, with birthdays, anniversaries, religious holidays, Father's and Mother's Days, visits from relatives, and so on, is very difficult. And there are "trigger" events—seeing a person or hearing a song that reminds you of the loved one. These go on for a long, long time.

Grief is a highly personal and
normal response to life-changing
events — a process that can lead to
healing and personal growth.

Reactions of others

We need the support of family and friends after a loss—companionship, understanding, practical help, a safe place to share feelings. How have people reacted to you since your loss? For example, who did you find helpful and supportive? Critical and judgmental? Who showed empathy and understanding? Who was smothering and overbearing? Did it feel like anyone pushed you to "get back to normal," or told you to be strong, or told you what you should do? Did anyone appear angry because you were crying too much, or too long, or because you were feeling down? Did you find anyone avoiding you? What happens inside of you when people react in any of these ways? Describe your feelings.

From loss to healing

Grief is the highly personal response to life losses. Let's look at *responses* for a moment. Responses are feelings, reactions, behaviors. When we grieve or mourn, the core feelings that are almost always present are powerlessness, fear, anger, and guilt.

Also present from time to time are feelings and behaviors such as shock, denial, disbelief, sadness, tears, sighing, searching, isolation, loneliness, depression, panic, apathy, frenetic activity, loss of appetite, overeating, sleeplessness, nightmares, and . . . the list goes on.

In other words, on the *inside* we might feel like we are going crazy. This is one of the most common expressions we have heard from bereaved people: "I thought I was going crazy."

Meanwhile, on the *outside*, certain definite but unwritten rules are taking effect. These rules come from friends, family, workplace, culture, and religion. Some of these rules are:

1. Don't talk about it.

2. Don't feel. That is, don't cry, don't show emotions.

3. Don't trust. This one originates inside the bereaved person when he or she accepts the first two rules. If I cannot feel or talk about it, whom can I trust with my feelings, my story, my urge to talk about my loss without fear of rejection or judgment?

4. Don't think for yourself. They know best. Who am I to question them? When we are grieving we can feel helpless about the loss. This feeling can expand to everything, and we can become vulnerable and open to others telling us what is good and right for us and not trust our own knowledge and instincts.

5. Don't change. This is the most dangerous rule of all. Change is threatening to those around us, because if we change then they will have to change. But if we don't change, we don't grow and if we don't grow, we die slowly but surely.

So there is pressure from inside—we are feeling crazy. There is pressure from outside—the rules. What do we do?

We must break the rules.

Talk. We must talk about our relationship with the deceased. We must review, reflect, and remember well the life, illness, death, and funeral of our loved one. We must break out of the imposed isolation and break the silence. Otherwise, we carry a terrible, burdensome secret.

Feel. We must acknowledge and express our feelings or else we become numb. Unexpressed feelings don't go away; they fester within our bodies and cause disease.

Think. We must begin to think for ourselves. A grief support group can help us to see what is "normal," to re-orient our thinking and doing, to give us a point of reference while we are feeling disoriented and lost.

Change and grow. We do have choices. We can choose not to risk, not to change, but we must remember that in doing so we are choosing not to grow, not to mature.

> *Life is change; growth is optional;*
> *choose wisely.*
>
> —Karen Kaiser Clark

> *Fears are educated into us, and*
> *can, if we wish, be educated out.*
>
> —Karl Menninger

Claiming your grief

Reclaim the power of *naming* and *knowing*. That is, if we can name our feelings, identify them, recognize them, and know them in some degree, we regain some of our power.

What feelings or reactions do you have right now about your significant loss? Name them out loud and list them below. If you need help finding the words, see the list on page 15.

_____

_____

_____

_____

_____

_____

_____

_____

_____

_____

_____

_____

_____

_____

_____

_____

_____

_____

_____

What unwritten rules do you identify with? Are there others?
List them below. How could you start breaking the rules?

_____

_____

_____

_____

_____

_____

_____

_____

_____

_____

_____

_____

_____

_____

_____

_____

_____

*Victory is won not in miles but in
inches. Win a little now, hold your
ground and later win a little more.*

—Louis L'Amour

Part II

Ten Steps
on the Road to Healing

Working Through the Steps

Part of healing is recognizing and expressing your feelings and completing unresolved issues with the person who has died. If you could do that in person it might be easier, but since that is impossible it is important for you to go through the process as if your loved one were present. This can be done through a series of rituals and exercises which will help you with the grieving process.

We strongly advise that you do your work with a partner, a trusted friend with whom you feel comfortable sharing. For some it might be even better to attend a grief support group with others who have experienced a recent loss. Whether you embark on this journey with a counselor, a friend, or with the support of others, it is important to schedule regular time for the work that is involved.

Remember, though, that this is your own personal journey towards wholeness, so move at your own pace. Try not to compare yourself to others. Each person is unique. Your answers lie within yourself. No one else's answers will fit you the way your own will.

It is important that some of this work end within the first year of your bereavement. It is only by resolving your issues and dealing with your emotions that you will feel ready or able to move on.

Exercises for awareness

In working through grief to recovery and healing it is important to experience our feelings. We often keep our feelings inside and avoid thinking or talking about the things that are painful to remember. But this only leads to further isolation and pain and the process of grief takes that much longer.

The exercises in this workbook are designed to help you safely draw your feelings to the surface so that you can move through them to recovery. Once you are aware of your feelings you will also begin to identify areas of unfinished business in your relationship with your loved one—unresolved feelings of guilt, perhaps, for things done and not done, a need to forgive and be forgiven.

It is important to allow yourself plenty of time to work through each step and to complete each of the exercises. It's a good idea to set up a separate space for this purpose, a special place that is quiet, where you won't be disturbed or interrupted. You might want to light a candle, a universal symbol of remembering. Or you might prefer to place a picture of your loved one where you can see it, or you might have another symbol that will help recall your loved one to you while you spend time on your workbook. Some people like to have music playing at this time. You will find whatever it is you need to do to separate and move inward from the busyness and noise of your outer world.

You might be tempted to go quickly from one exercise to the next. It is generally more effective to wait at least a week between steps to allow your feelings and insights to surface.

Rituals for working through grief

We need symbols in our life because sometimes words are not there to adequately express what we want to say. A ritual is an action performed in a symbolic way to make an inner event concrete. You can create a ritual that has meaning for you. Rituals can be performed alone, with your workbook partner, or in a group. Sometimes rituals are spontaneous, like listening to a favorite song or going to a significant place. A planned ritual could be a longer process.

There are many rituals you could create to help in your grief work:

- Telling the untold story in detail, noting the feelings as the story unfolds, and recording thoughts and feelings in a journal.

- Looking at losses in your past that may have remained unresolved.

- Releasing unshed tears, the outward expression of your deep inner feelings.

- Unlocking blocked anger, especially that directed at the deceased for having left you.

- Speaking unspoken words, saying unsaid goodbyes.

- Writing a letter to (or from) the deceased.

- Marking significant anniversaries, birthdays, and so on.

- Drawing a picture of your relationship(s).

- Forgiving the deceased for having abandoned you. Forgiving God for having taken your loved one from you. Forgiving yourself.

- Visiting the cemetery to say goodbye or to talk things over with the deceased.

- Letting go of the deceased, but honoring his or her memory with a symbol.

Suggestions for these and other rituals will be found in the Ten Steps. We also encourage you to create your own rituals so they will have special meaning for you.

We have provided space to record your work, to draw your thoughts and feelings, and to insert pictures and symbols for remembering. If you require additional space, we suggest you use your journal.

Before you begin

The steps we have outlined are guidelines only. Please feel free to vary and adapt them. If your loss involves the death of a loved one, we suggest that you complete Steps One through Five inclusive and then end with A Symbol for Remembering from Step Nine. Your grieving-healing process is what is most important. Silence is the prison, sharing is the key. Isolation and loneliness can be damaging to the soul. For this courageous journey we need encouragement from others. Our courage needs an encouraging environment in which to grow. If a counselor or friend or group does not provide an encouraging, safe place for you, keep looking until you find one.

Read through each exercise before you begin to write. Don't be concerned with perfect grammar or how well you express yourself. Try to express your feelings rather than simply describe events. Remember, this is for your eyes only, unless you choose to share it. And finally, try not to evaluate, judge, or analyze what you have written.

This workbook, although it focuses on grief at the death of a loved one, may be adapted to deal with any life loss. For example, the loss of a home or business; the end of a relationship; a change in work or career; a geographical move; a loss of trust, hopes, or dreams; the loss of dignity or self-respect through abuse, violation, or addiction—all of these are "deaths" that throw us into a mourning process. Remembering the past, redefining the present, and re-creating the future can serve as a helpful framework for dealing with any life-changing events.

God, grant me the serenity
to accept the things I cannot change;
courage to change the things I can;
and wisdom to know the difference.

—Reinhold Niebuhr

Remembering the Past

Step 1 The Life of Your Loved One

Step 2 Events Leading Up to the Death

Step 3 The Death

Step 4 The Funeral and After

Step 5 Your Grief

Unrecognized losses and unexpressed grief
are at the bottom of much of our unwellness.

—Fr. Jack McGinnis

Step One

The Life of _____

You are about to begin the difficult process called "grief work." In this first step, we will focus on the life of your loved one and your relationship with that person, no matter how long or short that may have been.

It is time to begin to tell your story, to review in detail all aspects of your relationship with the person you have lost and to deal with all the feelings that arise. It is time to recall and reflect upon the lifetime you shared. Using words, images, mementos, and symbols, you will portray what your relationship and life together was like. Be sure to express anger and disappointment along with the happy memories. If you find yourself feeling guilty, remember that your loved one is in a safe place now where expressing your words and emotions cannot upset him or her.

As you begin your grief work, you need to know that you may feel worse before you feel better.

Remember that this will be hard work, and that it is important to find a quiet space. Before you begin, pause for a moment and take a few deep breaths. You might want to relax with some music or just sit in silence. Be aware of the rhythm of your breathing as you take in the calm that surrounds you.

When you are ready, begin to work through the following exercises. In this first step, concentrate only on the life of your loved one and your relationship during that lifetime. Start by writing the name of your loved one in the blank space beside The Life of, above.

Silence is the prison; sharing is the key.

—Anonymous

It is important to be aware of what we are feeling at the moment. To recognize these feelings, it is helpful to name them. In a few words describe below how you are feeling at this moment. Be aware of fears, sadness, anticipation, peaceful feelings, relief, and so on.

_____

_____

_____

_____

_____

_____

_____

_____

_____

_____

Important milestones

In the space provided on the next page, list important milestones or events in the life of your loved one and in the lifetime you shared. Include as many as you can, both happy and sad. These might include marriage, conception and childbirth, childhood, adolescence, happy events, humorous happenings, celebrations, crises, and so on. (This may be a good time to go through some scrapbooks or mementos.)

Describe these milestones in as much detail as possible. It is important to write in the present tense and recall the feelings as if they are being experienced now, as you describe each event. As a way of becoming more aware of the feelings and insights of that time, you could add, "It is a time when . . ." For example:

We are celebrating our 25th wedding anniversary. All our family is gathering for the party our children have planned for us. It is a time when I feel deeply in love with John and afraid that we won't have many more celebrations together.

Describe the important milestones in your loved one's life and in your relationship.

_____

_____

_____

_____

_____

_____

_____

_____

_____

_____

_____

_____

_____

_____

_____

_____

_____

_____

_____

_____

Your relationship

Now describe with words, or draw a picture, image, or symbol of what your relationship was like with your loved one. Start by drawing something reflecting the wonderful, happy, positive aspects of your relationship. It might be a rainbow, a picture of a child in its mother's arms, or flowers, or abstract colors.

If you are working with someone, you might tell them what the drawing means to you or use this space to find the significance and meaning in what you've drawn. These questions can be used as a guide to help you remember some of the wonderful things about your relationship, or you can adapt these questions to any kind of loss. What were some of the things you giggled about? What did your loved one do to make you laugh? Were there special things you did that made your loved one laugh? Was there an interest or passion you shared? What were some of the favorite things you shared? What will you miss most? Did you confide in each other? How did your loved one influence you personally? How have you changed or grown as a result of being in this relationship? What did you learn from each other? How were your lives enriched by each other? Remember that each relationship is different and not all the questions will be relevant to your experience, nor should these questions suggest what your relationship "should have been like."

_____

_____

_____

_____

_____

_____

_____

_____

_____

_____

_____

_____

_____

Now use words, or draw a picture or symbol to describe some of the painful aspects of your relationship—any difficulties you experienced and any regrets you might have. Would the picture be a wall with each of you on different sides? Or perhaps an ice cube, expressing an absence of warmth and emotions, that perhaps will melt as time goes on and lead to healing? It might be a picture that shows great distance between you. Or it might be abstract.

Once again, describe the significance and meaning you find in what you've drawn. Often we grieve not for what was but for what might have been. What were some of the hopes and dreams you had for your relationship? What unmet expectations cause you to feel disappointed, angry, guilty, sad?

_____

_____

_____

_____

_____

_____

_____

_____

This is a very difficult part of the grieving-healing process. What could you do right now to nurture and take care of yourself?

_____

_____

_____

_____

_____

_____

_____

_____

_____

Mementos

Use this space to attach or to make note of any pictures or mementos that are particularly special for remembering the life of your loved one. Describe the memento's significance. Perhaps it's a piece of music that holds special meaning for you? If you are using a binder as a journal, you might want to add a pocket to hold these mementos.

Writing

Use the space below or a separate notebook to write or draw any feelings or insights that surface for you during the times between the Steps. Keeping a journal will help you track your progress (journey) through the grief experience from loss to healing.

Once you have finished, take a few moments to reflect about how you are feeling. Focus your attention on your breathing. Your breathing can become shallow when you experience strong emotions. Breathe slowly, deeply, and rhythmically to help relax.

It is likely that you have stirred up painful memories and intense emotions working through these exercises. You could feel exhausted, angry, or guilty even though you may also feel relieved and more at peace. Whatever you're feeling, remember it's okay. Be gentle with yourself. Remember to wait awhile before going on to the next Step. What could you do right now to nurture yourself?

Step Two

Events Leading Up to the Death

In this step we will focus on the circumstances and feelings surrounding the death of your loved one. When death has been preceded by a lengthy illness, it is especially important to include details and feelings about the hospital stay, the nurses and other hospital staff, and the doctors. Whatever the circumstances, you will probably begin to remember feelings of anger, guilt, frustration, and powerlessness. Areas of "unfinished business" may also surface.

Remember, grief work is a gradual, slow process. This is only a beginning. It will take some time to deal with these feelings. Be patient and be kind to yourself.

When you are ready to begin, take a few moments to relax. You may want to create a special routine or ritual to create the atmosphere for your work. This may include music, lighting a candle, taking a few minutes to concentrate on your breathing and just absorbing the peaceful silence, and quieting your thoughts as you move away from the busyness of the outside world.

"Why are you rushing so much?"
asked the Rabbi.
"I'm rushing after my livelihood,"
the man answered.
"And how do you know," asked
the Rabbi, "that your livelihood is
running on before you, so that you
have to rush after it? Perhaps it is
behind you, and all you need to do
is stand still."

—Rabbi Ben Neir of
Berdichev

Your feelings right now

Briefly describe how you are feeling right now. It is important to just note your feelings and not analyze them or judge them. Just let them be whatever they are.

_____

_____

_____

_____

_____

_____

_____

_____

_____

_____

_____

_____

_____

_____

_____

_____

_____

_____

_____

Your feelings then

Begin by reviewing, in detail, all aspects of your loved one's illness or circumstances leading up to his or her death. What were your feelings and reactions? Describe the feelings and reactions of your loved one. (You may need to use extra paper.)

Difficult feelings

Some people describe anger, guilt, fear, and powerlessness as core feelings in grief. Describe with pictures, words, or symbols any of these feelings that you experienced in the time before and leading up to your loved one's death.

These feelings are normal and often we avoid them because we feel so overwhelmed. Reflect on what you did to deal with your feelings. Did you talk to someone? Use a journal? Express them privately? Did you find yourself ignoring your feelings or denying them or pretending you really didn't feel that way? Were you upset with yourself for feeling that way?

Reflect on your relationship with your loved one in the time before he or she died. In the space below describe in as much detail as possible special moments or things said. Do you have any regrets for things that you did or did not say or do? What would you like to have said or done before your loved one died? Do you have any feelings of guilt? This is an important and difficult part of telling the story of your relationship.

_____

_____

_____

_____

_____

_____

_____

_____

_____

_____

_____

_____

_____

_____

_____

_____

_____

_____

_____

Unfinished business

Describe anything still unfinished as you reflect on the circumstances surrounding the death of your loved one.

_____

_____

_____

_____

_____

_____

_____

_____

_____

_____

_____

_____

_____

_____

_____

_____

_____

_____

_____

_____

_____

What are some of the things you'd like to say that weren't said or done?

_____

_____

_____

_____

_____

_____

_____

_____

_____

_____

_____

_____

_____

_____

_____

_____

_____

_____

Containing your grief

You may find yourself thinking about your loved one's death *almost all the time*. However, it is sometimes better to set aside a specific time for reflecting, drawing, and writing in your journal between the Steps. This may be easier said than done. But remember that you are engaged in difficult work. Try to resist the temptation to do it all at once.

How are you feeling right now? What will you do this week to nurture or care for yourself?

_____

_____

_____

_____

_____

_____

_____

_____

_____

_____

_____

_____

_____

_____

_____

_____

_____

Step Three

The Death

Step Three will focus on expressing feelings around your loved one's death. Your first reaction may have been to withdraw from the world. You may have experienced shock, an emotional cushion which provides layers of insulation so that reality can sink in slowly.

When feelings surface it is important to remember that they are neither right nor wrong, good nor bad. There is no need to label feelings; they are just there. They are ours and they need to be aired or else they fester and ferment and sour our personal lives. Or else we become numb, lifeless, unfeeling. Feelings are our energy source—they need to be expressed.

As you remember some of the details surrounding the death of your loved one, try to focus on your feelings both at the time and now as you reflect back. This is a very difficult step. Tears are normal and natural. You may have been trained that to be strong means not to cry. If so, try thinking of tears as a release of toxic waste, a necessary cleansing process of benefit to your whole body.

On learning of your loss

Describe what happened in the first minutes, hours, days. What do you remember feeling at the time? Can you remember people who were helpful or perhaps not helpful?

_____

_____

_____

_____

_____

_____

_____

_____

_____

_____

_____

_____

_____

_____

_____

_____

_____

_____

_____

_____

As you recall painful memories, many intense emotions might come up for you. Naming and knowing those feelings will make them less overwhelming or confusing. What emotions are you experiencing as you remember your loved one's death?

_____

_____

_____

_____

_____

_____

_____

_____

_____

_____

_____

_____

_____

_____

_____

_____

_____

_____

Difficult issues

Difficult issues often arise that need to be dealt with before and after the death of a loved one. Describe some of the issues that occurred, in as much detail as possible, using the issue of autopsy or the donation of organs for transplant as an example. What was the decision? Who made it? How did you feel about the decision at the time? How do you feel now? Were you faced with other issues? How were they handled? How do you feel now about how those decisions were handled?

_____

_____

_____

_____

_____

_____

_____

_____

_____

_____

_____

_____

_____

_____

_____

Continue to record thoughts and reflect on your feelings in your journal between the Steps. What have you been doing that has been healing for you?

Step Four

The Funeral and After

Step Four focuses on the burial rituals and customs of your religion or culture, such as the wake, funeral rites, cremation, burial, shivah, and so on.

There are so many feelings connected with grief—numbness, disbelief, denial, powerlessness, anger, guilt, fear, panic, depression, sadness, physical symptoms, and more—it is no wonder people feel as if they're going crazy. There are too many feelings to process all at once. Our emotional system is overloaded and needs numbness or denial for a while.

Inviting reality

Using the Ten Steps, you have been uncovering your feelings gradually and allowing reality to come to consciousness slowly. Step Four invites a bit more reality. However, awareness of reality and acceptance come and go. You may want to do certain things to encourage awareness and acceptance of your reality, things that others might perceive as crazy. However, it is often just what you need to do for yourself. Once you understand what it is you need to do, you are free to act upon it or not. For example, if you were not present for the funeral, you may need and want to create a ritual that is similar to a funeral. You may need to go to the cemetery and say some unsaid words.

Once again, prepare yourself and your space for the work you are about to do. Remember how important it is to tell your story in as much detail as possible. Describe how you are feeling at this moment.

_____

_____

_____

_____

_____

_____

_____

_____

_____

_____

_____

_____

_____

_____

_____

_____

_____

_____

_____

_____

_____

_____

Your loved one's body

Describe in as much detail as possible your experience of seeing your loved one's body in death for the first time. Did you touch him or her? Was the body buried or cremated? What was your reaction?

_____

_____

_____

_____

_____

_____

_____

_____

_____

_____

_____

_____

_____

_____

_____

_____

_____

_____

_____

_____

Your role in the rituals

Reflect on your feelings in the days immediately following your loved one's death. Use these questions as a guide. Who arranged the funeral? What part did you play in arranging the casket, the service, the burial? Describe your reactions during the wake, funeral, and at the cemetery (or other events, if you follow different customs). How did you feel about your role? About what was said by friends, relatives, clergy?

_____

_____

_____

_____

_____

_____

_____

_____

_____

_____

_____

_____

_____

_____

_____

_____

_____

_____

After the rituals

Numbness, disbelief, and denial can come in waves for a long time after the funeral and burial. People often need to go back to the hospital or the scene of the death just to make sure that their loved one is not there. Reflect on your feelings in the weeks that followed.

_____

_____

_____

_____

_____

_____

_____

_____

_____

_____

_____

_____

Journal Writing

Take a few moments before you end to check in with how you're feeling right now. If you wish, turn to your journal and note some of the emotions you are experiencing. Remember to breathe deeply.

Granted that I must die, how shall I live?

—Michael Novak

Step Five

Your Grief

The purpose of Step Five is to mark the beginning of a shift from expressing and understanding your feelings to more thinking and empowerment. Feelings are our energy base, our "e-motions," energy that propels us to motion, thinking, acting, doing, completing unfinished business.

As we realize the magnitude of our loss, feelings slowly return and break through the numbness. We enter a period of extreme emotional upheaval, often becoming consumed with feelings of grief and loss. Either from our experience as children or because of reactions from others, we may have learned not to "become emotional." To cope we may withdraw from our feelings, burying ourselves in activities. But it is important to acknowledge and accept our feelings and our loss in order to gradually let them go. This painful physical and emotional transition is the process of grieving.

You are not alone. Countless bereaved people describe feeling confused, overwhelmed, panicky; they express a desire to go to bed and never get up; some feel suicidal; many are in great pain. These are natural feelings. You are not crazy; you are in grief and these are the feelings of grief.

Core feelings of grief are powerlessness, fear, anger, guilt. Others include shock, disbelief, numbness, sadness, tears, depression, sorrow, loneliness, isolation, searching, panic, anxiety, frustration, sleeplessness.

When angry, count four;
when very angry, swear.

—Mark Twain

Expressing emotions

How did you express your feelings as a child? Were you allowed to cry? To show anger? Or did you have to hold back or even pretend that you were not feeling angry or sad?

_____

_____

_____

_____

_____

_____

_____

_____

_____

_____

_____

_____

_____

_____

_____

_____

_____

_____

_____

Which words describe how you are feeling now? Are there others you could add? Write a sentence about each one you are feeling.

_____

_____

_____

_____

_____

_____

_____

_____

_____

_____

_____

_____

_____

_____

_____

_____

_____

_____

_____

_____

_____

Breaking the rules

We are taught rules to follow when we experience the emotions of grief and loss. There are family, society, cultural, and religious rules. The rules that take over our responses are:

Don't Talk

Don't Feel

Don't Trust

Don't Think for Yourself

It is time to break these rules, whether they are self-imposed or imposed by others.

Break the Don't Talk rule. Talk to a trusted friend, counselor, or group. Choose wisely and carefully. Choose people you can trust not to give easy advice or quick comfort or criticize your way of grieving. Try not to isolate yourself.

Break the Don't Feel rule. Let your feelings out. Cry when you need to—find a place to do it. You may need a catharsis. Try listening to a piece of music or watching a sad movie. Don't try to be strong all the time. Give yourself permission to feel bad, depressed, sad, or angry at times, and then go back to getting on with your life.

Some people find it helpful to set aside some time each day to express their feelings of sadness, anger, or depression. Songs such as Barbra Streisand's "Memories," from *The Way We Were*, "Missing You," from *The Phantom of the Opera*, Bette Midler's "The Rose" and "Wind Beneath My Wings," from *Beaches* may provide a useful catharsis during a quiet time set aside for this purpose.

Break the Don't Trust rule. There are people who will say and do the wrong things. Many of them, relatives included, try to be helpful by spreading a veil of protective silence over IT. Choose trustworthy people with whom to share your story or feelings—people you can trust to listen to you and accept what you need to say and feel.

Break the Don't Think for Yourself rule. You may belong to a family, a social, or a religious group that pressures you to conform. Blind obedience is blind. Open your eyes and rethink what has been taught to you as a child. You are now an adult and can develop new responses and patterns. You can now think for your *self*.

If we never break any of the above rules, we run the risk of not changing, not growing. So, another rule is Don't Change or Don't Grow. Break it! Living involves change and growth.

How have you expressed your feelings of grief since your loss? What rules are having the greatest impact on you? How are they hampering or preventing you from talking, trusting, feeling, and thinking for your *self*?

_____

_____

_____

_____

_____

_____

_____

_____

_____

_____

_____

_____

_____

_____

_____

_____

_____

_____

_____

_____

Your trusted friends

Make a list of trusted friends with whom you can feel safe and can easily share your feelings and express your emotions; who do you want to tell what you're going through? Who among your friends and relatives are good listeners who will listen and understand without judgment? Who will offer support without "rescuing" or trying to "fix"?

Setting your own pace

While it is important to express your feelings, remember that you are in control of how much you want to say. It's okay to say "I feel sad right now," or "I feel confused. I don't have all the answers." Just saying it leads to enormous relief and increases your sense of control and self-respect because your feelings are important. They are not wrong.

Bereaved people often find it difficult to laugh again, to enjoy themselves without feeling guilty. Read the quote at the bottom of this page. How do you feel when you hear or see something comical? Do you think it necessary to appear sad all the time? Do you think people will judge you if you don't appear sad all the time? Do you judge yourself?

_____

_____

_____

_____

_____

_____

_____

_____

_____

_____

_____

I got the blues thinking of the future so I left
off and made some marmalade. It's amazing
how it cheers one up to shred oranges and
scrub the floor.

—D.H. Lawrence

Conclude this section by reflecting on how you are feeling right now. It is important to reflect on your thoughts and feelings and record them in your journal. Remember to keep in touch with your E-motions. They will give you the energy to break free of unhealthy rules that you, or others, impose upon yourself.

Before you continue

If your loss does not involve the death of a loved one, you may prefer to carry on and complete the Ten Steps in the order they are presented in this workbook. If you are in the first year after the death of a significant person in your life, some of the grief work suggested in the next Steps may be premature for you. After you complete the first five Steps, we suggest that you end your work for now with the section, A Symbol for Remembering, found in Step Nine.

Later, you can begin with Step Six and finish working through the rest of the Steps at your own pace. Why do we suggest this? People coming away from the death of a loved one, especially if they have cared for them after a long illness, are usually exhausted. They can only deal with a bit at a time. Moving on and letting go are action steps. It is very important for you to feel ready to move on before you continue. Grief work, remember, is a process and takes a long, long time.

And grieving is never really finished. We will have "unfinished business" right up until the moment of our own death, the time when we have to let go of all that appears important to us. Some people have described the whole life process in terms of a spiral pattern in which we go round and round at ever deeper levels. We do not exactly retrace our steps on each round but we tend to cover the same general turf and we encounter new experiences that help to shed new light on what it is to be a human being. So the idea that "Once I get through this I'll be okay and totally happy and perfect" just doesn't cut it.

Healing, the other side of grief, is a lifetime process. Please be gentle with yourself. Take a break if you need one. Then come back and do Steps Six through Ten when you feel ready. They are action steps leading to empowerment, your future, and your self-esteem. It is important not to put them off indefinitely.

You may even feel a real need to "get on" with your life. Some people may urge you to "get back to normal" as soon as possible. It is important to realize that you *are* getting on with your life and that the "old normal" is gone forever. This is a time of transition. It is a gradual moving towards the building of a new normal.

You may feel empty. Do not rush to fill up the emptiness. This is the neutral zone—a time of waiting. In the autumn the leaves fall from the trees and blanket the grass. There is a silence over everything. There is a stillness, a waiting period, a time to rest before new life appears again in the spring.

Redefining the Present

When I read this, I knew — as in really knew — that I was responsible for my life and that it would be the choices I made . . . that would determine the kind of life I had in the future . . . My doom was not sealed. My fate was not set. It was true that I could do nothing about what had happened, but I could do everything about how I continued to react to what had happened.

—Elizabeth Harper Neeld

Redefining the present

In some of the following sections, we refer to the death of a partner. If you have experienced a different type of loss—the death of a parent, child, or friend, or the loss of a relationship, job, health, or indeed, any other significant loss, the idea will be the same, and we encourage you to adapt the words and exercises to make them relevant to your situation.

Grief work is a process. Telling the story is only the first part. In this segment we move on from telling the story, recognizing our losses, and expressing our emotions, to focus on some of the tasks, actions, choices, and decisions that lie ahead as we build our life again. We refer to these tasks as:

1. Restructuring relationships

2. Liberating ourselves from bondage

3. Trapezing—holding on / letting go

4. Forgiving—ourselves and others

1. Restructuring relationships

Loss of any kind has an effect on all our relationships. For example, when a person dies, or leaves a relationship, the entire constellation of the household undergoes a change. On a very practical plane, the daily household tasks may need to be reassigned. Who, for example, cuts the grass? Who cooks the meals? Who does the shopping? Who sorts the laundry? Who takes out the garbage? Who writes the checks and pays the bills? Chances are, some of these duties may have to be reassigned now. Symbolically, and practically, someone else will likely have to take over some of the roles of the person who has died, or otherwise left the household.

2. Liberating ourselves from bondage

We become bonded to each other in our families of origin. When someone dies or leaves, what happens to the bond, the attachment? It doesn't just fade away. It lingers, and sometimes it can become a very tough umbilical cord holding us in "bondage" to the past. This type of "bond" is a form of imprisonment. We may be imprisoned by our guilt, our rage, our dependence, or whatever else might bind us to the past and hold us captive, preventing us from changing and growing in new and untried ways.

3. *Trapezing*

Let us look upon a trapeze artist as a symbol for both holding on *and* letting go. Although they are opposites, they are both of equal importance and connected, one to the other. We "trapeze" in our grief work by holding on to our memories, the legacy of goodness passed on to us, while letting go of whatever binds us and prevents us from moving on—such as guilt, resentment, or bitterness. Keep in mind that *we* are what connects the past to the future. We let go of one swing, trusting that we will grasp the next swing that will sweep us into a brand new experience. And keep in mind that trapezing is an art; it takes practice to find the rhythms that are right for us, and to gain the confidence to let go of one swing and take hold of the next at precisely the right moment.

4. *Forgiving*

Forgiveness, we believe, is an integral part of the grieving-healing process. However, it can also be one of the most confusing parts.

Many of us have been taught that before we can heal we must forgive the person who has wronged us. They may have wronged us. They may have abandoned us, disappointed us, or hurt us by actions taken or things said. To simply, "forgive and forget" somehow seems to trivialize the depth of our disappointment and anger.

Some people believe, however, that we don't have the power to forgive others. The best we can do is to forgive ourselves.

Still others believe that forgiveness is a moral value that comes from within us and that no one—therapist, friend, clergy—has the right to impose it upon us. We choose for ourselves if, and when, we are ready to forgive.

The spiritual leader Matthew Fox says that "forgiveness is another word for letting go" of the hurt, anger, resentment, and bitterness that are an inevitable part of loss. Kurtz and Ketcham in their book *Spirituality of Imperfection* describe the resentment as a poison that will isolate us as we continue to "go over an old injury revisiting the hurt, the powerlessness, the rage, the fear, the feeling of being wronged" and that only by forgiving ourselves can these feelings be released and we will heal.

Before you begin the exercises on Letting Go in Step Eight, reflect on your beliefs about "forgiveness." What does forgiveness mean to you? Is forgiveness making the choice to release feelings of bitterness or resentment, hurt, and disappointment? Does it mean transforming these feelings by accepting ourselves for being human and forgiving ourselves for feeling guilty and angry? What have your belief system and your personal moral values taught you about the concept of forgiveness? Have your beliefs changed as a result of your loss? In what way? Remember that there are no right or wrong answers to these questions. They are merely a guide to understand what feels right for you.

> *If you free what is inside you,*
> *it will make you free;*
> *if you hold onto what is inside you*
> *it will destroy you.*

> —Zen proverb

Step Six

Self-empowerment

Self-empowerment is the ability to see the possibilities and to freely make choices and decisions that will allow you to turn those possibilities into actualities.

In Step Six you will reflect on what unfinished business still needs to be done and what rules and beliefs still need to be broken, and you will choose the actions that need to be taken for self-empowerment to begin.

E-motional awareness

In John Bradshaw's work *Healing the Shame that Binds You* he makes reference to "e-motions" as "energy in motion." This is particularly true for anger. Anger is a force within us that moves us toward action. If we block our anger, we block our energy. Where does it go? Often it turns inward (implodes), becoming depression or causing illness. Sometimes it explodes into external violence or aggression. An "e-motion" is energy. It will have its day in court. It must express itself somewhere, somehow. There is a wise expression: "Express your feelings and you control them; repress your feelings and they control you."

So what do we do? We pay attention to our emotions, recognize and acknowledge them. They will give you the energy to break free of unhealthy rules that you impose upon yourself or others place upon you. At the same time, however, we do not have to allow them to run our lives, to block our opportunities to make new choices. In redefining the present, we can recognize and acknowledge our emotions and then move out of the emotion-based moment to a place of reason where we can make plans, choose, and decide.

What "e-motions" within you are imploding and could cause you inner distress or illness?

_____

_____

_____

_____

_____

_____

_____

_____

_____

What "e-motions" within you are exploding and causing trouble for you and others externally?

_____

_____

_____

_____

_____

_____

_____

_____

_____

_____

What do you need to do to get this "energy in motion" working for you rather than against your healing process?

_____

_____

_____

_____

_____

_____

_____

_____

_____

_____

Reality actions

"Reality actions" are some things you can do to allow denial to depart slowly and reality to sink in. Empowerment, our ability to move on, comes through actions and rituals. In this way, little by little, you will regain power and strength. It is important to set your own pace.

Go slowly. If you have dealt with illness over a long period you will be exhausted, drained, whipped. You need to take time to heal and regain your energy. This could take many months, even years. Therefore, be patient with yourself and try not to do too much too soon. Take a small step and then rest for a while. It is important for you to make up your own time frame. Others might express their opinions about a time frame based on their needs and experiences. You might want to consider what they are saying but remember that your grieving-healing process might be different and it is important to set your own pace.

The following are some suggestions of actions that others have found useful in moving through this process. If your loss did not involve the death of a person, reframe the statements below to make them relevant to your loss.

- Put away the belongings of your loved one. Keep what you wish and give away the rest. There may be friends and family who would appreciate something small as a memento.

- Prepare the deceased's room to be used by others.

- Place pictures of the deceased where you want them around your home.

- Talk to doctors and nurses and ask the questions you need to ask. Review the autopsy report with your doctor. You might take a friend with you. Get all your questions answered so that your imagination does not get out of hand. Find out the facts.

- Write letters to people who were important figures during this time.

- Arrange for a tombstone.

- Visit the cemetery. It is a place where you can say and do what you need.

- Return to the hospital or scene of the death. For example, a woman we will call Elisabeth returned to Children's Hospital a few months after her daughter had died. While her daughter was undergoing treatments for cancer, Elisabeth had lived at the hospital for weeks at a time. Afterwards, she attended her daughter's funeral and burial and ordered a stone to mark the spot of her daughter's resting place. But now she appeared at the hospital saying to us, "You won't believe why I'm here." She was embarrassed, and clearly worried that we wouldn't understand. "I just want to walk by my daughter's room," she said, "to make sure she's not there."

    Was she crazy? Not at all. She was doing a normal, natural thing for any mother. Was she in deep psychological trouble? Not in this case. She simply wanted some reassurance, some understanding, and some comfort from people who had offered support to her through the two long, hard years of her daughter's illness, people who had witnessed her ordeal and that of her daughter. She knew what she needed in order for her healing process to continue.

Periods of shock, denial, and disbelief can return during the grieving process and we need gentle "reality actions" to nudge us back on track again. Caregivers and counselors should not be too quick to overreact to such situations.

Actions already taken

What actions have you already taken to finish some of the business that needs to be done?

_____

_____

_____

_____

_____

_____

_____

_____

_____

_____

_____

_____

_____

_____

_____

_____

_____

_____

_____

Future reality actions

List some possible "reality actions" or tasks that are incomplete. It may be helpful to put dates beside each task—either when you will get started or when you will complete it.

_____

_____

_____

_____

_____

_____

_____

_____

_____

_____

_____

_____

_____

_____

_____

_____

_____

_____

_____

_____

End this section by reflecting on how you are feeling right now. Take some deep breaths. Be aware of any tension or feelings you are experiencing. Do you feel ready to go on with the next Steps?

You may want to wait for a while before undertaking some of the tasks facing you. It is important to wait until you feel ready, until your energy returns. And then, start slowly. You may want to put this workbook aside for days, weeks, or even months, and perhaps just continue your journal until you are ready to take the next Step. Give yourself permission to do so. *You* are in charge of your life. If you choose to put aside the workbook for a while, set up a time to check back with yourself to see if you are ready to get going again.

> *Power is strength and the ability to see*
> *yourself through your own eyes and not*
> *through the eyes of another. It is being able to*
> *place a circle of power at your own feet and*
> *not take power from someone else's circle.*

—Agnes Whistling Elk

Step Seven

Restructuring Relationships

The time has come to understand some of the changes that you are experiencing now that a relationship has ended. When a person dies, when a relationship changes or ends, in fact in any life loss when significant change takes place in our life, we lose not only the person (or thing) but we lose the *function* that person or thing served in our lives. A partner or friend might serve as a day-to-day helper, a social companion, a best friend and confidant, a soulmate. A child might connect you to other parents, a community, and your own playful self.

Relationships with friends and family may change. You may find that you have little in common with some of your friends. You may feel angry or disappointed by their attitude or behavior since your loss. You may find new interests that old friends don't share.

The role of your loved one

Describe the significant part or role that your loved one played in your life. For example, someone to go to a movie with, to share household tasks, to confide in, to rely on for advice, to share excitement with, someone to take care of and protect, someone to be silly with, someone to feel totally safe with.

_____

_____

_____

_____

_____

_____

_____

Describe the role that your loved one played with friends during his or her life.

_____

_____

_____

_____

_____

_____

_____

_____

_____

Describe the role he or she played in the family.

_____

_____

_____

_____

_____

_____

_____

_____

_____

_____

Describe now the significant part or role _you_ played in the relationship while your loved one was alive.

_____

_____

_____

_____

_____

_____

_____

_____

_____

_____

Describe the part *you* played in the family.

_____

_____

_____

_____

_____

_____

_____

Describe your role with friends.

_____

_____

_____

_____

_____

_____

_____

*No sooner do we think we have assembled a
comfortable life than we find a piece of
ourselves that has no place to fit in.*

—Gail Sheehy

Loss of your loved one's role

Describe the effect that the loss of your loved one's role or function has had on your life? For example, who shares the day-to-day responsibilities at home?

_____

_____

_____

_____

_____

_____

_____

_____

_____

What has been the effect on the family?

_____

_____

_____

_____

_____

_____

_____

_____

What has been the effect with friends? For example, are you still invited to get-togethers, movies, social activities with your friends? Do they treat you differently?

_____

_____

_____

_____

_____

_____

_____

_____

Is there a new role you would like to create with friends and family? If so, what would these new relationships be like? Remember, when we list possibilities we are just listing options. It doesn't mean we are obligated to fulfill them because they are written down. They are just a list of choices.

_____

_____

_____

_____

_____

_____

_____

_____

_____

Assessing relationships

When we experience a significant loss, relationships are likely to change. You may choose to continue to spend time with old friends or not. We usually do not have to give up the friendship, but often we have to change the dynamic. Sometimes we just need to open our eyes to look at relationships in a different way than before. Perhaps there is a new kind of relationship you could create.

How are you beginning to restructure your relationships? Make a list of the friends with whom you would like to create new relationships in one column, and next to the name of each person write the possibilities for what the new relationship could look like.

Name of friend	Possibilities

Grief's Courageous Journey: A Workbook

It is natural to become highly sensitive during the emotional grieving-healing process. Consider that your thoughts and feelings might be getting in the way of people trying to express how they feel about you as a person and a friend, or trying to contribute to your friendship. If you feel that some people are reacting differently to you than before your loss, you might ask yourself if there are any incorrect assumptions you could be making about what people are saying, feeling, judging, or thinking that are preventing you from enjoying and keeping their friendship. For example, you may think that friends are inviting you to a movie because they feel obliged to "take care of you," when really they just enjoy being with you and want your company. Do you have some indication based on conversation? Is there a way you could clarify this with them?

To examine this more carefully, list in three columns the names of friends, what they might be thinking, and other possibilities.

Name of friend	What they might be thinking	Other possibilities

Preparing for the new normal

You might wonder "When do I begin to laugh again without feeling guilty? When can I go out for dinner or to a movie? When will I be ready to go to a party, dance, celebration, or wedding? How will I handle my feelings when I go to the same hospital to visit a friend, or to the same funeral home where my loved one was?"

You can't know until you are actually in these situations or circumstances. Know, though, that however you respond is how *you* respond and that is perfectly normal. Which, if any, of these questions have "should" attached to them? Now is the time to let the "should" go. Who says you should, anyway? Remember, others may be entitled to their opinions, but they are not you. Only you know what is best and right for you.

In our work, we remind people that the word "should" is a clear indicator of guilt. At a time when it is so easy to be trapped in guilt, we often find that a bit of humor helps people remember this advice: "Don't 'should' on yourself; don't let anyone else 'should' on you; and don't 'should' on anyone else."

Anticipating special events

Are there any upcoming events (such as birthdays, anniversaries, special days) that will be difficult for you? Any events that will be difficult to attend? How are you planning for that time so that you can be gentle with yourself?

In the first column list events that will be coming up for you in the next few weeks. Beside each, in the next column, list any concerns that you anticipate, and then some possible actions you could take to deal with these concerns. This exercise can be used as often as you wish over the next several weeks, months, even years, as you face events and concerns.

Event	Concerns	Possibile actions

How could you reframe your attitude or thoughts so that this could be a positive experience? List some possibilities.

_____

_____

_____

_____

_____

_____

What are some of the things you can do now to take care of yourself as you experience anxiety about these approaching events?

_____

_____

_____

_____

_____

_____

_____

_____

It is easier to act your way into a new way of thinking than to think your way into a new way of acting.

—J.A. Davidson

Although the world is full of suffering, it is also full of the overcoming of it.

—Helen Keller

Step Eight

Letting Go

As you near the end of the Ten Steps, it is important to think about moving on, healing, letting go, and forgiving, but only when you feel ready to do so.

Forgiving yourself

Everyone has feelings of pain and anger for the way we might have wanted our loved one to be or not to be. Often we grieve not for what was but for what might have been. It is very important to forgive yourself for all the things you feel you have done that hurt or betrayed your loved one. If a little child spills milk or makes a mistake, you are likely to be compassionate and forgiving. Do you listen with compassion as friends berate themselves for something they have done? Do you extend that love and compassion to yourself? We can treat ourselves like a dear friend, reassuring ourselves that it's okay and telling ourselves not to be so hard on ourselves. We are likely to be much harder on ourselves than we are on others.

Also, remember that at a particular time a thought or feeling seemed appropriate, and it is only in retrospect that we question what we said or did, or a choice we made, and now feel guilty and regretful. We are not designed to be perfect. We are all human. Our task is to forgive ourselves, to let go of our bitterness and resentment. This is an important part of letting go. If we don't release these feelings, they can become toxic and continue to burden us.

Letting go

What does "letting go" mean? This phrase is often misunderstood. Does it mean forgetting, letting go of our memories? Not at all. Does it mean letting go of a relationship with our deceased loved ones? No! Our relationship is changed, not ended. "Letting go" refers to the time in our healing journey when we are ready to gently open our tightly closed fists. In doing so we let go of our pain. We do not need it any more.

Take both hands and close your fists tightly. Hold them closed as tightly as you can and then open them as wide as you can. Can you feel the difference as you open and let go? Can you feel the release?

We gradually realize that we neither need nor want what we have been holding on to—guilt, depression, sadness, anger, fear, powerlessness—whatever pain we have used as a connection to our loved one or as a way of protecting ourselves from further hurt. We might even make the decision that we will never, ever love someone again, so that when someone gets close to us, we do something to push them away. However, one day we may come to realize that we do not want or need this particular connection or protection. We have our memories and our bond with our loved one. In fact, to hold on to it fiercely would only ruin our lives. Our holding on would make us bitter, not better. This realization that we can, need to, want to, must let go of our pain is like watching the sun rise or set. It is a slow, gentle, almost imperceptible process that happens day after day, just as we will continue to release our pain again and again.

Letting go

What pain is protecting you or keeping you connected to the past?

_____

_____

_____

_____

_____

_____

_____

_____

_____

_____

_____

_____

_____

_____

_____

_____

_____

_____

_____

_____

_____

Make two columns. In one column list all the ways that your pain serves you. In the other make a list of all the things you are missing out on in life because you are holding on to fear, anger, guilt, and so on.

How my pain serves me	What I am missing out on

What connections with your loved one are keeping you from moving on with your life?

_____

_____

_____

_____

_____

_____

_____

_____

_____

_____

_____

_____

_____

_____

_____

_____

_____

_____

_____

Liberation from bondage

Those who have died need to be set free, to be released. Otherwise we make a "bond-age" out of what was the bond of the relationship both for them and for us. We have bonded to the ones we love; we must avoid turning it into bondage.

We are referring here to two words: "bond" and "bondage." A "bond" is defined in Webster's dictionary by a long list of words, including "anything that binds, unites, links, holds things together, connects." So we become bonded or united with our children, parents, friends, and siblings. A relationship begins at birth, and grows in our family of origin, and unites us for a lifetime. Bonding is like an invisible umbilical cord that attaches us to people, places, and things. So, what happens when someone we love dies? Or something we value is ripped out of our grasp—such as our health, our trust, our hopes, or our dreams?

The bond does not immediately disappear even though the imaginary umbilical cord is cut. It is like an amputee who still feels a phantom limb. The bond persists.

A bond becomes "bond-age" when it prevents us from moving on in life. Webster's defines "bondage" as "serfdom or slavery; subjection to some force, compulsion, or influence."

If a bond prevents us from moving on, then we are in bondage and we need to liberate ourselves. Otherwise, we are shackled to the past. It is as though we are walking backwards through life, unable to see or experience what lies ahead.

It can be a delicate and difficult operation to sever the bond, to cut the cord so that we can turn around and face life and reality once again. But remember, although we let go of the deceased and the past, we do not let go of our memories. They remain ours to enjoy forever. We let go only of the pain and any feelings we may have of guilt, or shame, or powerlessness, or fear. We let go of bitterness and resentment and rage, and in doing so we allow our dead, our past, to fly free.

This is a turning point because now we are ready to confront the question, "What do I want for me in my life now?" This may be particularly difficult for those of us who are accustomed to automatically taking our loved one's needs into account when making decisions. Now we may have only ourselves to consider, and that can be difficult.

Describe the bonds that connected you to the person who has died.

_____

_____

_____

_____

_____

_____

_____

_____

_____

_____

Have those bonds become bondage for you? If so, how?

_____

_____

_____

_____

_____

_____

_____

_____

_____

_____

How are you freeing yourself from the past and moving forward to a new life?

_____

_____

_____

_____

_____

_____

_____

_____

_____

_____

_____

_____

_____

_____

_____

Do not try to let go completely at this point. Letting go is one of the most difficult steps on our human, spiritual journey. It is a lifelong task, not a one-shot deal or a once-only opportunity.

Forgiveness is another word for letting go.

—Matthew Fox

Ways of letting go

- Write a letter to the person who has died, saying all you need to say. Then burn the paper and scatter or bury the ashes, symbolically letting go. You may wish to light a candle and keep it beside you as you write. When you are finished and ready to let go, blow it out. It might be important to have a trusted friend take part in this ritual to provide support.

- Wait awhile before burning your letter and write a letter back from your loved one letting you go. Have a burning of both letters and let the wind scatter the ashes.

- Write whatever you want to let go of and draw a circle around the words you have written. Draw a line from the circle to the edge of the page. Now imagine that you have just drawn a balloon and you are going to let it go.

- Burn a symbol of your pain, of your holding on, of your anger, guilt, or control, and allow the air to waft the smoke skyward.

- Bury a symbol in the ground.

- Put a symbol in a balloon and let go of the balloon.

- Go to the cemetery or a place that holds meaningful memories from your life together and say goodbye.

For example, Gerry and his wife had gone through a painful divorce. He had grieved for all that he had lost—his best friend, their relationship, and all the hopes and dreams they had shared. Their special place was a log cabin nestled in a beautiful woodland overlooking a stream, where they had spent many wonderful hours. It was the only tie left, and now it was up for sale. He invited some of his men friends to the cabin to help him with his ritual of letting go, for saying his final goodbye. They lit a fire and each man took a turn speaking of what he knew of the couple's life together. Finally Gerry spoke. Then they lit sage and sweetgrass and took the smoke from room to room to cleanse the space and honor the happy memories that he would always have. With the support of his friends, he left for the last time.

Remember, you are letting go of your pain, your hurt, your unforgiveness, whatever is holding you back from living, changing, and growing. You are not letting go of your memories or your relationship with your loved one.

Warning

by Jenny Joseph

When I am an old woman I shall wear purple
With a red hat which doesn't go, and doesn't suit me.
And I shall spend my pension on brandy and summer gloves
And satin sandals, and say we've no money for butter.
I shall sit down on the pavement when I'm tired
And gobble up samples in shops and press alarm bells
And run my stick along the public railings
And make up for the sobriety of my youth.
I shall go out in my slippers in the rain
And pick the flowers in other people's gardens
And learn to spit.

You can wear terrible shirts and grow more fat
And eat three pounds of sausages at a go
Or only bread and pickles for a week
And hoard pens and pencils and beermats and things in boxes.

But now we must have clothes that keep us dry and pay our rent
and not swear in the street
And set a good example for the children.
We must have friends to dinner and read the papers.

But maybe I ought to practice a little now?
So people who know me are not too shocked and surprised
When suddenly I am old, and start to wear purple.

Reprinted by permission of the author.

Re-creating the Future

Those who bear the mark of pain
are never really free, for they owe a
debt to the ones who still suffer.

—Albert Schweitzer

Re-creating the Future

We "re-create" the future (not merely "create" it for the first time) because our expectations, hopes, and dreams have been altered. We created it once and now must re-create it because of our loss. So in a sense we are re-creating something from the ashes of the old—almost like the phoenix bird rising from the ashes, a transforming death-resurrection process.

Step Nine

The Legacy

A symbol for remembering

Think of a "symbol for remembering" your loved one. Examples might be a picture, a poem, a stained glass memento, the planting of a tree, or the setting up of a memorial plaque or fund.

It is important to have mementos—memories and reminders such as letters, pictures, words, sounds, songs, or anything that reminds you of your loved one. Actions and rituals (symbolic actions) may remind you, too—planting a tree, donating to a special charity or fund, placing an anniversary notice in the paper, having a mass or saying a prayer in memory, lighting a candle, providing an annual scholarship, making a stained glass symbol for your home, or having a special Christmas ornament. Remember that the healing process can be impeded by not remembering well.

Use the space below to describe the symbol(s) or memento(s) you have chosen, and their significance. You may find it helpful to review what you wrote in the section on mementos on page 37 of this workbook and in your journal.

Slowly we can begin to recognize, acknowledge, and accept the legacy of goodness passed on to us by those who have gone before us. This legacy of wisdom and goodness is now ours to embody and to use for the sake of our world. Erich Lindemann, M.D., Ph.D., called this the "component of resurrection" in the grieving process. It is up to us, the survivors, to raise up the goodness of our predecessor friends and relatives and pass it on to our corner of the world. Goodness grows.

When someone dies we bury the body, which is the shell that housed the essence (spirit) of that person. But what about the gifts, that special goodness, that each person brings into the world? It is important not to bury their goodness with their bodies.

Our loved ones have left a legacy as models, guides, and teachers to those of us left behind. In recognizing that continuity, we are aware that the real legacy is not the worldly possessions willed to us, but the nonmaterial gifts that have been left, the truths by which our loved one has tried to live, and the values they leave for those to follow.

We learn from facing death something about how to live. Write a will from your loved one in your notebook describing the nonmaterial gifts that they have left for you and for others. You may wish to use the guided imagery exercise below to help you with this exercise.

What legacy have you received as a result of your relationship? How has your loved one's memory affected your life, your values? What are some of the nonmaterial gifts that he or she has left you? For example, you may have learned how to face adversity with courage from your loved one. Or you may find yourself responding to a situation with a sense of humor that you know you "inherited" from your loved one.

Guided imagery

The following exercise will be the most effective if you observe a few simple guidelines. First, you should be reasonably awake and alert; do not try the exercise when you are fatigued or it may do more harm than good.

Second, make yourself as physically comfortable as possible in a seated position; if you lie down, you may drift off to sleep. Take off your shoes, jewelery, and watch; loosen your outer clothing. Make sure you will be undisturbed by any possible intrusion or distraction for at least the next half hour.

As you breathe in, feel the energy you are taking in fill your being with vitality. As you breathe out, feel all the wastes and toxins accumulated throughout your body dissipate. Let your muscles relax in every part of your body as you become aware of your growing relaxation and calmness.

Now imagine that within your sanctuary you are standing on a path that stretches off into the distance. You start to walk up the path, and as you do so, you see in the distance a form coming toward you, radiating a clear, bright light.

As you approach each other you begin to see whether the form is a man or woman, how he or she looks, how old he or she is, and how he or she is dressed. The closer he or she gets, the more details you can see of face and appearance.

Greet this person. Notice the wisdom and the love that are in the face and eyes of this person; wisdom and love that are there just for you now.

This person knows you well. He or she has an important and helpful message to give you, a message to guide you in your present life. Perhaps this message relates to an issue you are aware of, or perhaps it relates to one that has not yet crossed your conscious mind. Wordlessly, the person gazes at you with understanding and communicates this special message through direct eye contact with you.

Listen to what this person has to say to you. Listen to any advice he or she has to give you. If you wish, you can ask some specific questions. You may get immediate answers, but if not, don't be discouraged; the answers will come to you in some form later.

Before you leave, notice that your guide has a gift for you. Reach out and receive that gift. This gift will help you in your healing.

When the experience of being together feels complete for now, thank your guide, express your appreciation, and ask him or her to come to meet you in your sanctuary again. Remember, you can visit this place, so quiet and so beautiful, anytime.

When you are ready, open your eyes and return to the present. If you choose, begin to write about your experience in your workbook or journal.

_____

_____

_____

_____

_____

_____

_____

_____

_____

_____

_____

_____

_____

_____

_____

*Sometimes I go about pitying myself, and
all the time I am carried on great winds
across the sky.*

—Ojibway

Step Ten

Opening the Door

There's a saying that when one door closes, another opens. Sometimes we can't see the new opportunities right away.

In the past we might have made choices based on the needs of our loved one, or our responsibilities to the family, or our work. Now is an opportunity to discover some of our own strengths, interests, and dreams to guide our new choices in the future. If we are to make new choices, it is important to stay open to what is possible in our lives.

New opportunities

What doors do you see opening for you? What choices? How would you like to design your future?

_____

_____

_____

_____

_____

_____

_____

_____

_____

_____

_____

_____

_____

Make a list of all the activities that are fun or interesting to you, that feed your spirit and give you pleasure.

_____

_____

_____

_____

_____

_____

_____

_____

_____

_____

Who, among your friends, might be interested in doing some of these things with you now?

_____

_____

_____

_____

_____

_____

_____

_____

_____

_____

Your support system

Who is part of your support system as you embark on this new phase of your life? Make a list and beside each name, indicate what they can offer in support of what you want to do now. For example, who will encourage you and affirm your efforts and victories? Who might be interested in trying new things with you? Who can remind you of all the things you always wanted to do? Who will cheer you on if you become discouraged?

Your fears

Choosing new activities and interests and changing old patterns takes work, intention, and awareness of all possibilities. Sometimes, when emotions well up, or it all seems too difficult, fear can overcome us—fear of what the future holds, fear we won't make it, fear of more pain—and we might shut down and become discouraged again and again. This might call up feelings of guilt, frustration, even unworthiness. But remember the old adage that says "We create what we fear." So if we're afraid to learn something new, we won't try and we, in fact, will not learn something new. There's another old adage that says "There's nothing to fear but fear itself." We recommend a book called *Feel the Fear and Do it Anyway* by Susan Jeffers (Ballantine Books,1987). Even if you don't read the book, it can be helpful just to remember the title!

It is important at this time to live in the moment rather than too far in the future. Uncertainty almost always raises fears and insecurities that can hold you back. What fears still hold you back?

_____

_____

_____

_____

_____

_____

_____

_____

_____

_____

_____

_____

_____

Your needs

Remember to attend to your whole *self*—the needs of the emotions, the mind, the body, and the spirit. What are you doing for your self?

_____

_____

_____

_____

_____

_____

_____

_____

_____

_____

_____

_____

_____

You have now completed the Ten Steps from loss to healing. Spend some time reviewing your experience and how important it has been for you to do your grief work.

We hope you have gained insights, grown in unexpected ways, dealt with emotions, and resolved issues with which you have struggled. Perhaps you have found a "new normal"—new choices, new patterns, and new experiences. It is important to be aware that intentions can direct the way we act and that we don't have to let life just happen to us. *We can be intentional. We do have choices.*

New hopes and dreams

For this exercise imagine that it is one year from today. Imagine that you are meeting a friend that you haven't seen during the past year. Tell your friend all about your life, what's happened since you last met, what new things you are doing, how you are feeling, if you are working or have changed jobs, or had a promotion. Tell your friend if you have moved, either within the same city or to another area. Be sure to record this "conversation" on tape or on paper, for it is your blueprint. It contains important clues about your hopes and dreams for the future. This could be a good exercise to do with one of your supportive friends.

_____

_____

_____

_____

_____

_____

_____

_____

_____

_____

_____

_____

_____

_____

_____

_____

Closing exercises

Hindsight produces insight. As you look back over your life losses reflect on some of the clarity and insights that have come to you.

_____

_____

_____

_____

_____

_____

_____

_____

_____

_____

_____

_____

_____

_____

_____

_____

_____

_____

_____

This next exercise is intended to help you integrate the insights from your previous workbook exercises with the way in which you want to live your life.

Lie down or sit in a comfortable place. Close your eyes and take two or three deep breaths. Move inside yourself and go back over the time since you began the Ten Steps. Be aware of significant highlights. (Maybe a conversation with someone, or a particularly powerful experience.) What have you learned?

When you are ready, turn to the next page and write at the top of the left column *What I have learned* and at the top of the right column *What I intend*. In the left column write down what you have learned during the Ten Step process. Then, beside each learning, write down your intention; that is, how you intend to act on the basis of this learning. For example, you might have learned that it is important to tell special people in your life how you feel about them. Note this in the left column. In the right column you might write "Tell my mother and children I love them. Send them a card." That is your intention. By being specific, it will be easier to know whether you have followed through with your intentions. At the same time, it is also important to be realistic with yourself.

What I have learned	*What I intend*

Healing through helping

There is healing in helping others. As Henri Nouwen wrote in *The Wounded Healer*: "Shared pain is no longer paralysing but mobilising." Consider ways you can now support others because of your experience with loss and grief. List them below.

_____

_____

_____

_____

_____

_____

_____

_____

_____

_____

_____

_____

_____

_____

_____

_____

_____

Celebrating life

There will still be tears and feelings of sadness as you recall your life
loss. These feelings will gradually be replaced at times with joyful
memories. Grief work is never really finished. Each goodbye from
now on will bring back feelings of loss and loneliness. You have
worked hard and faced your grief courageously. It is time now to
celebrate life once again. How might you celebrate the progress and
the changes you have made?

_____

_____

_____

_____

_____

_____

_____

_____

_____

_____

_____

_____

_____

The open door

You are moving on to a new place in your life—an opportunity to
make new choices and to discover new possibilities. Having completed your list of intentions, you might want to lie back, turn on
some music (preferably a piece without words), and imagine a door.

Note what the door looks like. Is it large or small, painted or wood, old or new? Where is the door? (Is it a gate in a fence? A church? A home?) Where does the doorway lead? Is there a window? Is it clear or opaque? What do you see through it? Is anyone there? What are they doing? When you are ready, use your workbook or journal to write some of your thoughts and insights.

_____

_____

_____

_____

_____

_____

_____

_____

_____

_____

_____

_____

_____

_____

_____

_____

_____

_____

_____

Part Three

Starting a Grief
Support Group

The Facilitator's Guide

Introduction

We have written this guide for people who want to facilitate a small support group for those who have experienced a significant loss. This guide is designed to be used in conjunction with the workbook that precedes it. The guide follows a step-by-step program developed over a ten-year period and adopted by the London chapter of Bereaved Families of Ontario.

Because there are many excellent leader's guides and books on how to set up self-help support groups, we have focused on group leadership principles and structures that we have found effective for grief work. We encourage you to expand our suggestions as you design a program based on your own experience.

The self-help/mutual support process

Self-help support groups bring people together who share a common experience or problem and provide a safe place where members can talk about their loss, share their story, and express their grief. Through the self-help process, they no longer feel alone or unique. They feel hopeful as they see how others have coped, and learn about their grief as a normal response to loss. Members find a network of caring people building trust and relationships, and find comfort in knowing that others understand what they are going through. But the real benefit of self-help lies in the principle that as we help others, we help ourselves.

The structure of mutual support/self-help groups is often followed in grief support groups, but we have made some changes in our model.

	Mutual Support/ Self-Help Group	Grief Support Group
Frequency of Meetings	weekly / monthly	weekly
Duration	long-term	usually time and size limited
Registration	none	preregistration required
Leadership	relies heavily on peer leadership	usually a professional or specially trained lay facilitator who has experienced a grief support group
Agenda	flexible	more structured format
Scope	strong social component often with some education/ advocacy	combines education about the normal process with opportunity to do grief work

Structure of sessions

There are many formats for grief support groups. It is important to choose one that best fits the needs of the members and the skills of the facilitator. The format will give structure to the work that the group is doing and help create a safe environment. Support groups are usually small (6 to 10 people) and each meeting usually lasts for two hours. For example, the first part of the session—the welcome, opening, and checking in—could be about 25 minutes, the discussion topic could take 75 minutes, the break could be 5 minutes, and the closure could be 15 minutes. We recommend that the structure of each session includes:

1. **Welcome:** to greet each member as they arrive.

2. **Opening:** to help people let go of the day's events and enter into the process of the meeting. This could be a short reading, a poem, or a few focusing words from the facilitator.

3. **Check-in:** to go around the circle (including the facilitator) and give people the opportunity to share an event from the week, to focus on how they are feeling, and to just "get there" and leave the busyness of the world outside.

4. **Topic:** a reading from a book or article followed by a discussion, or a topic for the evening, such as those suggested in the Ten Steps section of the accompanying workbook, or Harriet Schiff's *Living Through Mourning*, or Westberg's *Good Grief.*

5. **Brief break:** for coffee, tea, or bathroom.

6. **Closure:** to review without opening any new areas. Wind down and check with each person to see how they feel at this point. Introduce topics for next week and suggest work they might do at home (exercises from the workbook, journal writing).

The structure we have outlined can be changed and adapted to meet the needs of group participants. Grief work is a highly personal process. Some people avoid groups and prefer to do the work by themselves or one-on-one. It is important not to judge the choice made. What is important is that people choose what will help them through their grieving-healing process.

We usually find that the first five Steps are completed within the first year after the loss. If the loss is a life loss other than death, individuals alone or in a group may prefer to do the Ten Steps in the workbook in a sequential series of sessions with a counselor, therapist, good friend, or small support group.

If the loss is the death of a loved one, then we suggest the following for a small grief-support group: a "veteran's" night, Steps One to Five inclusive, an open forum session to discuss anything the group wants to bring up, and a final session to deal with endings and goodbyes. (We suggest you choose either the Symbol for Remembering exercise from Step Nine or the Open Door exercise from Step Ten for the closing exercise.) The group then would have had at least eight sessions together. Then we suggest you take a break.

We suggest a break at this point because people who have experienced the death of a loved one, especially after caring for them during a long illness, are usually exhausted, emotionally and physically drained. They can only deal with their grief work a bit at a time. They often need time before they are ready to begin the difficult work of letting go and moving on. So we suggest to them to do some work now, some later. Then, when they are ready, we suggest that they come back to complete Steps Six to Eight and repeat Steps Nine and Ten. Letting go and moving on to a new phase in your life are action steps and take a lot of energy. Grief work, remember, is a process and takes a long, long time.

Some participants from small support groups have set up monthly meetings (called Family Nights) after they end their small group sessions. These nights are for the bereaved, for family members, professionals, and others who might be interested. These meetings might include educational events about grief for the public, social or fund-raising events, and provide a place for newly bereaved people to meet others and find out about the small grief support groups. There is usually some sharing of experience, strength, and hope, but Family Night is not meant to replace the small, more intense, time-limited grief support group.

Room setup. Sitting in a circle helps create a "barrier-free" environment—no tables, and so on, and helps people make and keep eye contact. A circle offers support to the person speaking or sharing feelings and encourages greater participation and listening.

Refreshments. To help people feel welcome and relaxed, tea and coffee can be served during and after the meeting. This will encourage informal sharing.

Role of the facilitator

The word "facilitator" means to make easier. In a grief support group, the facilitator's task is to create a safe environment that makes it easier for group members to tell their story, express their feelings, and share issues of concern. A facilitator leads by encouraging members to participate and share as openly as they can. Each session is structured so that focus is on the group and each member, rather than on the leadership of the facilitator.

The facilitator's role is to:

- Welcome group members
- Create a safe, comfortable environment
- Remind people of the ground rules

- Introduce focus for the evening
- Maintain the focus and keep the group on track
- Introduce "veterans" at first meeting
- Demonstrate and guide check-ins and closure

Both professionals and trained lay facilitators can work effectively with grief support groups. We have found that people with basic skills in group leadership and some experience with groups have more confidence and are better able to lead groups. We suggest that facilitators take a leadership training program and, if possible, go through a grief work program before beginning to facilitate a group alone.

If a group includes both men and women, we recommend male and female co-facilitators.

Creating a safe environment

Many people feel uncomfortable in groups, and may hesitate to speak or express feelings. Coming to a group, especially if you feel vulnerable, can be frightening, and people need reassurance that they will not be hurt further by what happens at meetings. How safe and accepted members feel will affect their ability and willingness to participate. People will share their story only if they are assured of a safe, confidential environment where they find trustworthy people.

Some ground rules are needed to establish a safe place:

- Everything we say is confidential.
- We will listen as one person speaks.
- We will wait in silence when a person expresses feelings or emotion.
- We will not judge anyone or what they say.
- We will not compare our story adversely with anyone else's.
- We will not discount anyone's loss or feelings.
- We will not give advice.
- We will not speak for another person.
- We will not interrupt, interpret, or talk over each other.

Members may want to add other ground rules.

Role of the veteran

Modeling is another way to encourage group participation. "Veterans" are people who have participated in grief support groups and have agreed to introduce a new group to the grief process in the first session. They attend the first meeting only and share the full story of their loss with the new group members. They bring a picture of the person who died and tell the story of their relationship—the life, death, funeral, and after.

As the veterans share their experience, strength, and hope the newcomers often express a sigh of relief, because at last they have discovered someone who has walked in their shoes. And they gain hope from the veterans—"If they made it, maybe I can too."

Veterans are usually chosen for a specific group according to their losses; i.e., if the newcomers are parents of a Sudden Infant Death Syndrome (SIDS) child, a SIDS veteran couple will be chosen, and so on.

Veterans provide an excellent start for a newcomer's group. As they tell the full story of their loss, they model what the whole process is about, show how grief work is done, and share their sorrows and joys, their tears and laughter, their moments of despair and their hopes.

The workbook

This facilitator's guide has been written for use in conjunction with the workbook that precedes it. We suggest that each group member have his or her own workbook and do the exercises in each Step between meetings. Some people will share their experiences with the group, while others may feel uncomfortable or unable to write down or share what they've written. You can encourage them to try, but it is important to respect each person's right to choose not to do so.

Preliminary Session

Veteran's Night

Purpose

Veteran's night is a session in which bereaved persons who have already experienced a grief support group come to a preliminary meeting with a newly formed grief group. The veterans share their "story" and how they did their grief work, to encourage new members to participate in the upcoming sessions.

Welcome   *(about 30 minutes)*

- Begin with a warm welcome to all and thank them for coming. Reassure participants that this will be a safe place to do the difficult process of grief work. Begin to create a sense of trust by describing the ground rules for a safe place (see page 125).

- Outline the topics you will explore during your sessions together and the format you will follow for each meeting.

- Before introducing the veterans, ask each person to introduce themselves and very briefly comment on why they are present. Veterans should be included and the leader should provide a model by introducing him- or herself first.

Topic   *(about 75 minutes)*

- Introduce veterans. Using pictures, the veterans talk about their deceased loved ones, sharing their experience, strength, and hope.

- Answer questions from newcomers.

- Ask for a commitment from newcomers to the series of meetings.

Brief Break

Closure

- To check in and wind down ask each person, "How are you feeling?"

- Introduce next week's topic: The Life of Your Loved One. Ask new members to bring a picture of the deceased for next week's meeting.

- Ask if everyone can be present for next week's meeting. If they have a workbook, they could begin Step One in preparation for next week.

Session 1

Step One: The Life of Your Loved One

This group session will help members begin sharing their relationship with the person who has died. Using a favorite picture, they will review and reflect upon aspects of their relationship from beginning up to but not including the time of illness or death.

Welcome   *(15 minutes)*

- Begin with a warm welcome to all. Thank them for coming and repeat how difficult this process of grief is—that's why it is called grief "work." It is hard work.

- Remind them of last week's process in which the veterans told the whole story of their loved one. Tonight they are making only a start by reviewing, with the help of a favorite picture, some aspects of their relationship up to the time of illness or death. So, their focus tonight is on the life of their loved one, no matter how short or long their relationship with that person was.

- Before the sharing do a brief check-in with each person by asking, "How are you feeling tonight, _____?" Let each know that the group is willing to listen to a longer answer than a mere "fine," which is often our customary answer out there, outside this group.

Topic   *(90 minutes)*

- Ask one person to begin with his or her picture. Remind each person that they have about 15 minutes and repeat that the focus is on the life of the deceased. That may include conception, pregnancy, birth, naming, baptism, childhood, adolescence, and so on, covering as many incidents or circumstances of the relationship as they remember and have time to share tonight, up to but not including the illness and death.

- If there are people who share on the same loss (parents with the death of a child), each person should share his or her own relationship with the deceased.

- The picture is usually passed around the group for a closer look. Participants should avoid comments. This time is reserved for the one telling his or her story.

- At the last session you asked participants to bring one or two favorite pictures. If they could not choose and brought scrapbooks instead, let the participants look after the session; otherwise the group gets distracted flipping through the pictures.

This session is usually an enjoyable experience because people begin seeing, recalling, and recounting memorable and even humorous events that they may have temporarily forgotten.

Brief break

Closure   (15 minutes)

- Ask each person, "How are you feeling?"

- Check to see if anyone needs a ride home or needs company for the drive.

- Ask if everyone can be present for next week's meeting. Ask them to use their workbook to remember other details of the life of their loved one.

- The next session's topic is the illness or circumstances surrounding the death of each person's loved one. Those whose loss was by sudden death may want to continue reflecting on details of the person's life or begin work on Step Three, dealing with the death.

Session 2

Step Two: Events Leading Up to the Death

The purpose of this session is to allow participants time to begin reflecting upon the illness or circumstances of the death of the loved one.

Welcome (15 minutes)

- Begin with a warm welcome to everyone. A reminder that this is a safe, confidential place can be repeated from time to time.

- Ask each person, "How are you feeling?" Take a few minutes with each person.

Topic (90 minutes)

- Remind the group that the focus of tonight's remembering is on the illness or circumstances of the death of the person for whom they are grieving. It is very important for survivors to share some of their feelings about doctors, nurses, hospitals, and all the circumstances of and feelings about an illness. But there is no way in 15 minutes that they can share everything—all the feelings of anger, guilt, frustration, and powerlessness, and the "unfinished business" that may surface at this session.

- Note that tonight is only a beginning for sharing details, aspects, and feelings, and that not everything can be uncovered or dealt with tonight. It is a beginning.

- If there are people present who faced the sudden death of a loved one, a death that involved no illness, ask them to be patient with those who had to deal with a long illness. Their sharing tonight can continue their focus on the life of the loved one, or they may want to begin to reflect upon the death of the loved one.

- Ask people not to go into detail about actions they may wish to take against hospitals, doctors, or various systems and institutions, but rather to begin uncovering their feelings about the illness. Action about unfinished business will come later in the sessions.

- It is inevitable that religious issues come up at some time in the sessions. We suggest that they not be discussed or dealt with any sooner than Step Four, and preferably not until one of the last sessions.

Brief break

Closure   *(15 minutes)*

- Check with each person to see how he or she is feeling.

- A brief relaxation exercise may be helpful before participants leave.

- Remind everyone that the next session's focus is on the death of the loved one—a particularly difficult session. Encourage people; they are doing difficult work.

- Encourage them to use the workbook between sessions and to take some time to reflect on the death of their loved one. They should set aside an hour or two—a specific time for their reflection—and then put the workbook away rather than dwell on it all week long. This is easier said than done.

Session 3

Step Three: The Death

The purpose of this session is to focus on sharing feelings about the death of a loved one.

Welcome *(15 minutes)*

- Welcome everyone warmly. Remind them again that this is a safe place "in here" as opposed to "out there." Some people describe the group as a haven.

- Note that feelings are neither right nor wrong, good nor bad; there is no need to label feelings. Our feelings exist and may need to be aired. If we stuff them away they may ferment and sour our lives. Or we might become numb and lifeless—unfeeling. Feelings are our energy source; they need to be expressed. Express your feelings and you control them; repress your feelings and they control you.

- Check in with each person: "How are you tonight?"

Topic *(90 minutes)*

- Remind participants that the focus tonight is on the death of their loved one; not so much the details surrounding the death but on their feelings at the time, and now as they reflect upon that event. Allow 15 minutes for each person.

- Note that this is a difficult night, that tears are normal and natural for us as men and women, human beings that we are. We may have been trained to be strong and not to cry. We need to revamp our thinking. Tears may be seen as a release of toxic waste. If we don't release them, they become toxic to our bodies.

- Someone has named tears "liquid anger." Core feelings in grief are powerlessness, fear, anger, and guilt.

Brief break

Closure *(15 minutes)*

- Ask each person how he or she is feeling.

- Remind them that they may not have a good night's sleep after some of these sessions. If people drive together from a distance, they usually continue the dialogue all the way home, and later report that this was an excellent process. Some may wish to go out together after the sessions for coffee and talk.

- If they wish to share phone numbers, encourage them to do so.

- Encourage them to continue writing in their workbook and journal.

- Remind them that the next session's work will focus on the wake, funeral, and burial.

Session 4

Step Four: The Funeral and After

The purpose of this session is to allow participants to review their feelings about the wake, funeral, and burial of the deceased.

Welcome (15 minutes)

- Check in with each person: "How are you tonight?"

- Remind people that there are many feelings connected with grief—numbness, disbelief, denial, powerlessness, anger, guilt, fear, panic, depression, and sadness, as well as physical symptoms. No wonder people sometimes feel like they are going crazy! There are too many feelings to process all at once. Our emotional system can get overloaded and needs numbness or denial for a while.

- What we are doing together in these grief support groups is uncovering our feelings gradually, and slowly letting our consciousness come up to reality. Tonight is a bit more of reality.

- However, awareness and the acceptance of reality comes and goes. For example, wanting to go to the cemetery in winter and put a blanket over a child's grave is not crazy or unreal. It is a real, protective feeling, and we can choose to do whatever seems right for us at the time, regardless of what people "out there" may think. The time this group spends together is time for sharing what may appear crazy to people out there. Once we have shared our feelings, we are free to act upon them or not.

Topic (90 minutes)

- Focus on feelings about the wake, funeral, and burial of the deceased.

- When religious or spiritual issues are raised either in this session or a later one, remind the group that it is important to listen to each person's opinion and beliefs in this highly personal area, without judging or giving advice. The group is not a place for arguments, proselytizing, or converting others. Listening to each person and honoring his or her story and pain provides the safe place for this work to be done.

Brief break

Closure   *(15 minutes)*

- Check with each person. How are they now? How are they feeling about the sessions?

- Encourage them to use the workbook between sessions.

- Ask if each person can be present next week.

- The next session moves into the area of feelings—all the feelings that the participants mentioned earlier (or, if you wish, they could be mentioned here).

Session 5

Step Five: Your Grief

The purpose of this session is to provide a forum, a safe place where participants can discuss what they are feeling and thinking as bereaved persons who have suffered a significant loss.

Welcome *(15 minutes)*

- Check in with each person: "How are you tonight?"

- Review Breaking the Rules (don't talk, don't feel, don't trust, don't think) from Step Five of the workbook.

Topic *(90 minutes)*

- This session is the beginning of a shift from feeling towards thinking and empowerment. Feelings are our energy base, our "e-motions," energy that propels us to movement, motion, thinking, acting, doing, and completing unfinished business.

- Ask participants to describe rules that have had an impact on them and how they have been hindered from talking, feeling, trusting, and thinking for themselves.

Brief break

Closure *(15 minutes)*

- Leave participants with the question, "What actions can you take to break the rules?" Remind them to keep in touch with their feelings, their "e-motions," because that will give them the energy to break free of the unhealthy rules imposed by others and by themselves.

Remind people in their first year of bereavement to check in with the group. If they feel ready to go on, continue with Steps Six through Ten. However, it is often preferable to let some time pass before doing these steps.

If so, we suggest two sessions after Step Five. The first, an open forum session, could allow for participants to discuss any topics, concerns, and questions they have. It might be helpful to make a preliminary list of concerns raised by the group to see common areas and cover as many of them as possible in the session.

In the final session, we suggest you ask them to bring a symbol for remembering. We suggest you use the Symbol for Remembering exercise from Step Nine or the Open Door exercise in Step Ten in this concluding session.

This final session is held for endings, symbols for remembering, and goodbyes that may be difficult but are important. A verbal or written evaluation of the sessions for feedback can be included now or by mail later. Affirmations of the group for the work well done are also an important component of this session.

If you decide to shorten the number of sessions, the format would look like this:

Session One: Veteran's Night
Sessions Two through Six: Steps One to Five inclusive
Session Seven: Open Forum
Session Eight: Endings

People using this workbook to deal with life losses other than the death of a loved one or people working through the grief process one-on-one with a counselor or good friend may not feel the need to take a break and may decide to continue on together to complete Steps Six to Ten.

Session 6

Step Six: Self-empowerment

The purpose is to give participants an opportunity to discuss and reflect on emotions that may be working for or against their healing process. They can discuss what unfinished business needs to be done and what actions need to be taken so that self-empowerment can begin.

Welcome   *(15 minutes)*

- Check in with each person: "How are you?"

Topic   *(90 minutes)*

- Ask each person to share how he or she is handling emotions. Which emotions are giving you energy? Draining you? Which emotions are imploding? Which are exploding? How?

- What actions have you taken to finish some of the business that still needs to be done? (See workbook.)

- Remind them to go slowly. If they have dealt with a long illness and then a death, they may have been in this for some years and will be exhausted, drained, whipped. They need to take time to heal and regain their energy. This may take years, depending on the length of the illness. Therefore, they must be patient with themselves and not try to do too much too soon. Suggest that they take a small step and then rest for a while. Urge them to make up their own time frame.

Brief break

Closure   *(15 minutes)*

- The next session's topic is restructuring relationships.
- Can everyone be present next meeting?
- Ask participants for feedback about the sessions? There are four more to go. Are they looking forward to them? Feeling anxious?

Session 7

Step Seven: Restructuring Relationships

The purpose of this session is to provide a time and place for participants to discuss their feelings about the ending of a relationship as well as the loss of the deceased person's "function" in the family. What does this mean now? How might a restructuring of relationships look?

Welcome *(15 minutes)*

- Check in with each person. "How are you?"
- Watch for upcoming anniversaries, birthdays, and special days such as Mother's Day, Father's Day, etc.

Topic *(90 minutes)*

- Read the workbook section in Step Seven about "should" and "should not." Discuss.
- Ask each person to share the following: 1) How has your life changed since your loss? 2) What function or special part did your loved one play in your life, in the life of your family, and with friends?
- Go around the circle again, addressing the question: What are some of the possibilities for creating new relationships with the same friends?

Brief break

Closure *(15 minutes)*

- Check in with each person before they leave.
- Ask if they will be present at the next session.
- Ask whether there are any upcoming events that might be difficult—birthdays, anniversaries, etc.

- Check to see whether the group might like to do something different next week, such as watching the movie, *Always*, which depicts "letting go" in a different way.

- Remind them to read and work on their own in the workbook.

Session 8

Step Eight: Letting Go

The purpose of this sesion is to give participants a safe forum in which to think and talk about healing, moving on, letting go, and forgiving and, if they are ready and willing, perhaps take a first step. Religious/spiritual questions may also be discussed.

Welcome   *(15 minutes)*

• Check in; ask each person how they are.

Topic   *(90 minutes)*

• Be aware that the format of this meeting may vary depending on which ideas (suggested below) the participants and facilitator(s) choose to pursue.

• Explain that letting go does not mean forgetting. In all these sessions participants have been remembering. It is essential that we remember our loved ones, our past relationship with them, and our present relationships.

• Ask the participants to consider what a relationship with the deceased person looks like. The movie, *Always*, with Richard Dreyfus, Holly Hunter, and Audrey Hepburn (1989) could be a good starter for discussion on this topic. Or participants may use their nondominant hands to draw a picture of their present relationship with the deceased. Ask them to discuss their own pictures.

• Discuss the question of forgiveness and how it is relevant to each person's grieving-healing process. Remind the group not to judge others.

• Consider the quotation from Kubler-Ross, "Let your dead fly free." Ask what might keep them from letting their past "fly free."

• Read the section from the workbook about trapeze artists. Then ask what life losses they have had that have helped them with the art of trapezing.

- If the group is open to it, lead a discussion regarding spiritual questions. What happens when we die? Where do we go? How do we communicate with loved ones after death? Discuss any religious questions that arise. (Remind the group to listen to each other's opinions and beliefs in this area with respect and to share without proselytizing or arguing over personal religious beliefs.

Brief break

Closure   (15 minutes)

- Ask participants to think about a symbol for remembering their loved one. This could be a picture, a stained glass memento, the planting of a tree, the setting up of a memorial plaque or fund, and so on. Ask them to bring the symbol to the next meeting or, if this is not possible, to come prepared to talk about what symbols for remembering they already have or are contemplating.

Session 9

Step Nine: The Legacy

The purpose of this session is to focus on the legacy of wisdom and goodness inherited from your loved one or from your experiences of loss, tragedy, and suffering. Symbols for remembering your loved one and mementos to keep memories alive are an important part of this step.

Welcome   *(15 minutes)*

Topic   *(90 minutes)*

- Ask each person to share his or her symbol for remembering and its significance.

- Hindsight produces insight. As you look back over your life losses, share some of the clarity and insights that have come to you.

Brief break

Closure   *(15 minutes)*

- Remind people that the group sessions will end after the next meeting.

- Acknowledge that endings are usually happy and sad as people feel the loss of the group while looking forward to the future.

- Ask the group how they would like to spend their last session together. A shared meal, a social, a meal at a restaurant, or some ritual to help symbolize their time together and the need to say goodbye.

- Hand out evaluation forms to be completed at home and brought to the final session.

Last Session

Step Ten: Opening the Door

The purpose of the last session is to give participants time to talk together about the doors of opportunity that are opening for them now, to be affirmed in the work they have done individually and together, and to say goodbye to each other. This session could last longer than previous ones, depending on what exercises are done and whether a shared meal or ritual is included. An option is to have the shared meal or ritual another time.

Welcome (15 minutes)

- Check in; ask each person how they feel tonight.

Topic (90 minutes)

- Make time for each person to reflect on and express his or her appreciation for the program. Collect evaluation forms handed out at the previous session.

- Briefly affirm each person's progress in his or her grief work. This can be done in the group, but focus on one person at a time.

- Use the Open Door exercise to discuss each person's next step. Remind people that changing patterns that we are used to takes time. It is a time for patience, for being good to ourselves, and for taking one step at a time.

- Goodbyes can be in the form of a shared meal, a ritual, or a symbolic leave-taking. For example, the group can form a small circle of chairs and take two minutes to focus on one person at a time. Participants may then say what they wish to affirm this person's presence in the group or to recall something especially meaningful that happened between that person and the participant giving feedback. Comments could end by wishing him or her well in the future.

Some Other New Harbinger Self-Help Titles

Scarred Soul, $13.95
The Angry Heart, $13.95
Don't Take It Personally, $12.95
Becoming a Wise Parent For Your Grown Child, $12.95
Clear Your Past, Change Your Future, $12.95
Preparing for Surgery, $17.95
Coming Out Everyday, $13.95
Ten Things Every Parent Needs to Know, $12.95
The Power of Two, $12.95
It's Not OK Anymore, $13.95
The Daily Relaxer, $12.95
The Body Image Workbook, $17.95
Living with ADD, $17.95
Taking the Anxiety Out of Taking Tests, $12.95
The Taking Charge of Menopause Workbook, $17.95
Living with Angina, $12.95
PMS: Women Tell Women How to Control Premenstrual Syndrome, $13.95
Five Weeks to Healing Stress: The Wellness Option, $17.95
Choosing to Live: How to Defeat Suicide Through Cognitive Therapy, $12.95
Why Children Misbehave and What to Do About It, $14.95
Illuminating the Heart, $13.95
When Anger Hurts Your Kids, $12.95
The Addiction Workbook, $17.95
The Mother's Survival Guide to Recovery, $12.95
The Chronic Pain Control Workbook, Second Edition, $17.95
Fibromyalgia & Chronic Myofascial Pain Syndrome, $19.95
Diagnosis and Treatment of Sociopaths, $44.95
Flying Without Fear, $12.95
Kid Cooperation: How to Stop Yelling, Nagging & Pleading and Get Kids to Cooperate, $12.95
The Stop Smoking Workbook: Your Guide to Healthy Quitting, $17.95
Conquering Carpal Tunnel Syndrome and Other Repetitive Strain Injuries, $17.95
The Tao of Conversation, $12.95
Wellness at Work: Building Resilience for Job Stress, $17.95
What Your Doctor Can't Tell You About Cosmetic Surgery, $13.95
An End to Panic: Breakthrough Techniques for Overcoming Panic Disorder, $17.95
Living Without Procrastination: How to Stop Postponing Your Life, $12.95
Goodbye Mother, Hello Woman: Reweaving the Daughter Mother Relationship, $14.95
Letting Go of Anger: The 10 Most Common Anger Styles and What to Do About Them, $12.95
Messages: The Communication Skills Workbook, Second Edition, $13.95
Coping With Chronic Fatigue Syndrome: Nine Things You Can Do, $12.95
The Anxiety & Phobia Workbook, Second Edition, $17.95
Thueson's Guide to Over-the-Counter Drugs, $13.95
Natural Women's Health: A Guide to Healthy Living for Women of Any Age, $13.95
I'd Rather Be Married: Finding Your Future Spouse, $13.95
The Relaxation & Stress Reduction Workbook, Fourth Edition, $17.95
Living Without Depression & Manic Depression: A Workbook for Maintaining Mood Stability, $17.95
Coping With Schizophrenia: A Guide For Families, $13.95
Visualization for Change, Second Edition, $13.95
Postpartum Survival Guide, $13.95
Angry All the Time: An Emergency Guide to Anger Control, $12.95
Couple Skills: Making Your Relationship Work, $13.95
Stepfamily Realities: How to Overcome Difficulties and Have a Happy Family, $13.95
The Chemotherapy Survival Guide, $11.95
The Deadly Diet, Second Edition: Recovering from Anorexia & Bulimia, $13.95
Last Touch: Preparing for a Parent's Death, $11.95
Self-Esteem, Second Edition, $13.95
I Can't Get Over It, A Handbook for Trauma Survivors, Second Edition, $15.95
Dying of Embarrassment: Help for Social Anxiety and Social Phobia, $12.95
The Depression Workbook: Living With Depression and Manic Depression, $17.95
Prisoners of Belief: Exposing & Changing Beliefs that Control Your Life, $12.95
Men & Grief: A Guide for Men Surviving the Death of a Loved One, $13.95
When the Bough Breaks: A Helping Guide for Parents of Sexually Abused Children, $11.95
When Once Is Not Enough: Help for Obsessive Compulsives, $13.95
The Three Minute Meditator, Third Edition, $12.95
Beyond Grief: A Guide for Recovering from the Death of a Loved One, $13.95
Leader's Guide to the Relaxation & Stress Reduction Workbook, Fourth Edition, $19.95
The Divorce Book, $13.95
Hypnosis for Change: A Manual of Proven Techniques, Third Edition, $13.95
When Anger Hurts, $13.95
Lifetime Weight Control, $12.95

Call **toll free, 1-800-748-6273**, to order. Have your Visa or Mastercard number ready. Or send a check for the titles you want to New Harbinger Publications, Inc., 5674 Shattuck Ave., Oakland, CA 94609. Include $3.80 for the first book and 75¢ for each additional book, to cover shipping and handling. (California residents please include appropriate sales tax.) Allow four to six weeks for delivery.

Prices subject to change without notice.

About the Authors

Sandi Caplan is a counselor in private practice in London, Ontario. A graduate of the University of Western Ontario, she has spent the past 20 years in the health care field, where she has developed a variety of support programs for individuals, families, and professionals. In 1980 she received the Lifestyle Medal from Health and Welfare Canada for her pioneering work in establishing the Heart to Heart program for cardiac patients and their families. A member of the Canadian Association for Pastoral Education and founding president of the Hospice of London, she has served on the board of Canada's National Self-Help Directorate and as a committee member for the Professional Advisory Committee of Bereaved Families of Ontario (London Chapter), the Bereavement Ontario Network, and the National Patient Services Committee of the Canadian Cancer Society.

Gordon Lang has worked in adult education, grief counseling, and pastoral care for over 35 years. A member of the Canadian Association for Pastoral Education, he pioneered grief support groups for bereaved families at the Victoria Hospital and St. Joseph's Health Center and assisted in the founding of Bereaved Families of Ontario (London Chapter). A graduate of the University of Western Ontario, he has led workshops in Canada, the U.S., and Ireland, and he currently teaches a course on "Healing the Inner Child" in the University's continuing education program. Semiretired, Gordon spends his time teaching, grief counseling, conducting retreats, and watching his granddaughter grow.